Production

Management

About the Author:

William R. Puckett

For the more than thirty years, Bill has held senior engineering and management positions encompassing a variety of manufacturing and distribution environments. His management style has been instrumental in achieving validated and unparalleled manufacturing performance achievements and establishing new industry benchmarks. Bill has an exceptional record of organizational and human research, consulting, and training. He has conducted numerous seminars on human performance and behavior within the working environment.

Production Management:

Our mission is to deliver on-time, with quality excellence, at the lowest possible total cost.

1. **Quality Assurance Process Structure:** (Page 5)
    a. Definition of structure,
    b. QA process documentation management,
    c. Validation of raw materials,
    d. Validation of specifications, work instructions, and samples,
    e. Confirmation of line and work place configurations,
    f. Work-in-process audit / validation of assembly conformance,
    g. End-item audit and final validation,
    h. Corrective action management,
    i. Data analysis and reporting.

2. **Staffing Calculation Level Projection:** (Page 27)
    a. Client partnership and communication,
    b. Branch partnership, support, and communication,
    c. Projection of weekly volume forecast,
    d. Definition / identification of daily production volume requirements,
    e. Projection of efficiencies,
    f. S.A.M.'s / production standards definition,
    g. Calculation of staffing projections,
    h. Communication of needs.

3. **Production Order Management:** (Page 41)
    a. Client communication and order prioritization,
    b. Definition of start / end parameters,
    c. Definition of on-time targets and thru-put time,
    d. Design and maintenance of high-visibility control board,
    e. Tracking and communication of production schedule performance,
    f. Supervisory / lead / associate accountability.

4. **Production Flow Management:** (Page 50)
   a. Projection of staffing levels,
   b. Confirmation of raw materials supplies,
   c. Confirmation of equipment availability,
   d. Operational work flow balance (theory of constraints),
   e. Effective planning and execution of shift start-up,
   f. Planning and execution of next-order set-up,
   g. Performance manager / supervisor / lead / materials coordinator accountability.

5. **Associate Performance Management:** (Page 78)
   a. Definition of ideal associate profile,
   b. Appropriate screening and selection of production associates,
   c. Methods training and work pace hardening,
   d. Individual / team / line hourly production goals,
   e. Management of effective associate work pace,
   f. Coaching and positive reinforcement,
   g. Decision Making / Corrective action management.

6. **Work Place / Line Structure for Maximum Economy:** (Page 94)
   a. Definition and understanding of product construction,
   b. Work place arrangement for accuracy, efficiency and safety,
   c. OHIO,
   d. Standing verses sitting,
   e. Cross-training,
   f. Empowerment to address the constraint,
   g. The shortest distance between two points (I's, U's, L's, J's, C's, N's),
   h. Continuous improvement.

7. **Identification & Training of Best Methods:** (Page 107)
   a. Management, supervision, and engineering define methodology,
   b. Define best methods and practices . . . who and where are the highest levels of total accuracy and productivity,
   c. Train the best methods and practices . . . mentor training,
   d. Positive reinforcement of progress and achievement,
   e. Continuous improvement.

8. Positive Reinforcement / Celebrate Success: (Page 113)
   a. Effective establishment and communication of appropriate key performance indicators (KPI's) / critical success factor goals,
   b. Establish cognitive dissonance . . . track and communicate actual performance verses goal,
   c. Set up the win . . . celebrate success!
   d. Raise the bar,
   e. Do it all over again!

Quality Assurance Process Structure

1. Quality Assurance Process Structure:

a. Definition of Structure,

"**Quality is the inevitable result of good management.**"

W. Edwards Deming

As we commence with any initiative or endeavor relative to total productivity, it must be recognized that the most inefficient manner to do anything is <u>over again</u>! Numerous and broad industry based studies by such individuals as W. Edwards Deming, Phillip Crosby, and Bryan Joyner have shown repeatedly that the cost ratio of performing work consistent and correctly the first thing (DIRTFT is the acronym for "Do It Right the First Time") verses over again (re-pair, re-work, re-make, re-inspect, re-process, re-bate, etc . . . . . . any and all of those "re" words) is 1 to 5. In other words, for every $1 spent in doing things right the first time, it requires $5 to do it over again! This additional cost is an accumulation of labor, materials, overtime, scrap, management / administrative costs, diminished efficiencies, revenue loss, delayed or missed shipments, customer dissatisfaction, and market share erosion. Depending upon the specific product, market, customers, and other factors, the costs associated with doing things over again may actually be higher. While it is well recognized that total operational perfection is not possible, it is incumbent upon all in management and engineering to seek to find what Mr. Deming refers to as the "optimum economic balance" in relation to all operating structures and associated costs.

As various operating platforms are assessed relative to the operating structure and accuracy requirements, the "optimum economic balance" or most effective ROI relative to our quality assurance costs must be ascertained. Depending upon the specific operating conditions relative to de-containerization / sortation / palletization, order picking, product assembly, re-packaging, or machine cell operation; in conjunction with product / service output conformance parameters, tolerances, and service level requirements, a quality assurance structure is designed and deployed. While basic, fundamental structures and management accountabilities relative to the quality assurance remain consistent, specific operational and technical aspects require adjustment and/or modification in regard to the specific operating environment wherein the program is being deployed.

The basic or fundamental structure of the significant majority of the process control systems and structures remain relatively consistent. They consist of:

    i. Accuracy and communication of product and/or service requirements,

    ii. Accuracy and communication of work instructions,

    iii. Consistency and validation of raw materials and components,

    iv. Functionality of work place and/or line structures to consistently yield prescribed requirements,

    v. In-process sampling and process data analysis to assure accuracy of execution,

    vi. End-item auditing and product data analysis to assure conformance to customer requirements of delivered products and/or services,

    vii. Focused corrective actions in regard to opportunities surfaced in pursuit of continuous improvement.

Total Quality Assurance Process Map:

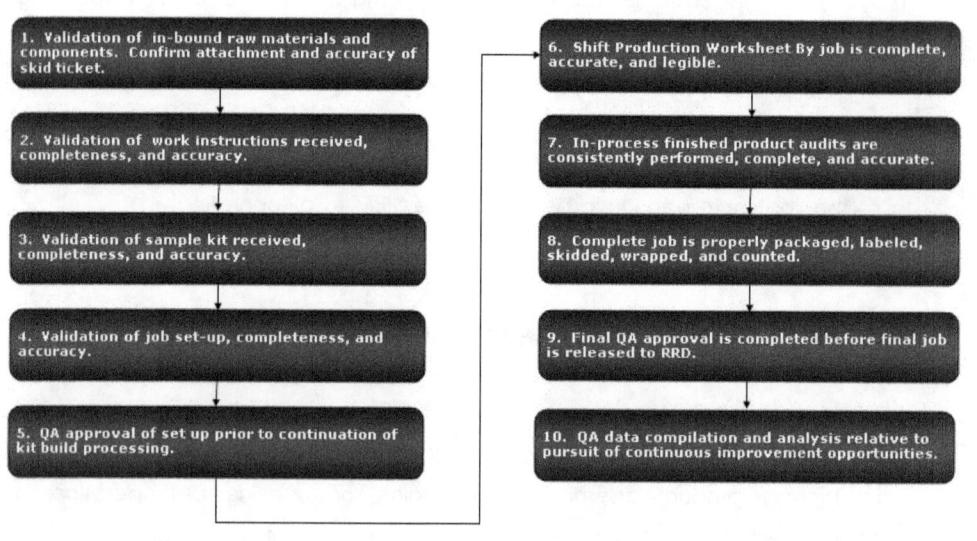

As noted in the following example for the Gap, the largest apparel retailer in the U.S., a fundamental structure with specific modification for the operational environment within the assigned area of Staffmark / Output Solutions has been designed, approved, and is undergoing deployment.

Quality Assurance Process:

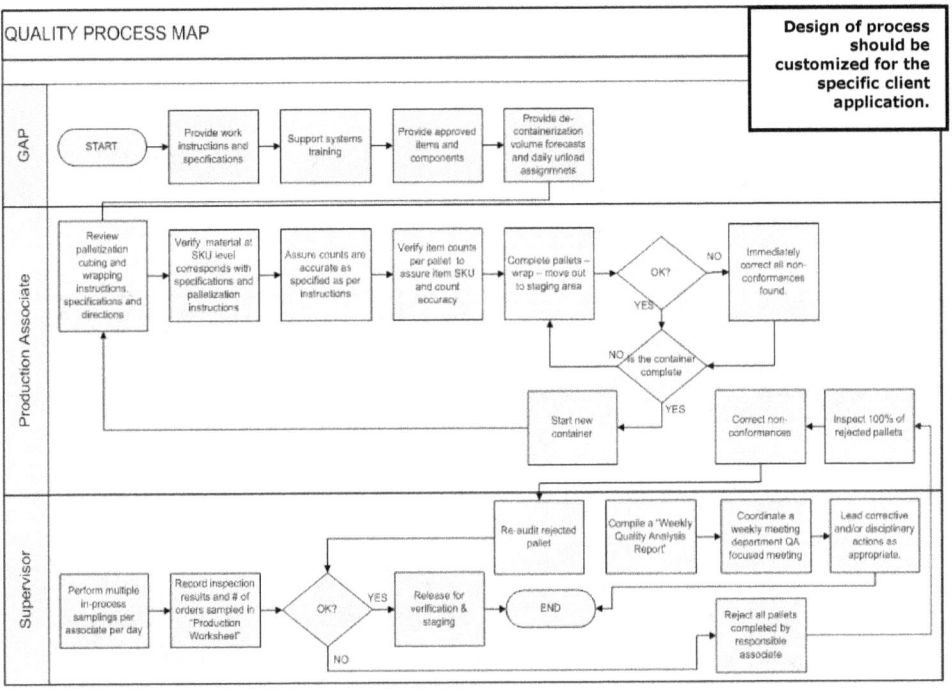

The above process, as designed and deployed, has proven to yield a cost-effective process control system that delivers sustainable performance relative to customer-based parameters and requirements in regard to product and/or service accuracy, consistency, and conformance.

As these QA structures are designed, deployed, and consistently maintained, the overall effectiveness of the comprehensive quality assurance approach will be significantly enhanced in regard to achieving conformance excellence relative to meeting the client's requirements the first time, every time, on-time.

b. QA Process Documentation Management:

> "One cannot manage what one does not measure."
>
> Peter Drucker

As John Kenneth Gailbraith so well said, "It is almost as important to know what is not serious as to know what is." It is only through our thorough collection and effective analysis of qualitative and quantitative production observation data and comparison of that data in relation to definable product and service requirements and parameters that we truly know where to best focus corrective actions and process improvement initiatives for optimum results.

The significant majority of in-process and end-item observations are collected on a daily basis via the daily or shift production work sheet (DPW). The daily production worksheet provides an excellent tool for the supervisor, lead, and/or in-process auditor to observe and collect conformance data.

Designed more specifically for dedicated in-process sampling at higher levels, the following worksheet provides intensive focus and data collection at the product, job, production order, shift, team, line, operation, and individual levels.

In-Process Audit Data Collection Worksheet:

> Design of forms and data collection should be customized for the specific application

AUDITOR: _____ **CUSTOMER:** _____

SUPERVISOR: _____ **MANAGER:** _____

#	Associate:	# Units Inspected:	# Errors:	Error Type(s):	Time:	Date:	Shift:	Line:	Operation:	Product:	COMMENTS:
1					:						
2					:						
3					:						
4					:						
5					:						
6					:						
7					:						
8					:						
9					:						
10					:						
11					:						
12					:						
13					:						
14					:						
15					:						
16					:						
17					:						
18					:						
19					:						
20					:						
21					:						
22					:						
23					:						
24					:						
25					:						
26					:						
27					:						
28					:						
29					:						
30					:						
31					:						
32					:						
33					:						
34					:						
35					:						
36					:						
37					:						
38					:						
39					:						
40					:						

This data, in turn may then be compiled and analyzed by major defect classification, shift, team, line, product, or individual, whatever means that will provide the greatest visibility into specific areas of focused, concerted activity in regard to corrective actions and forward improvement opportunities that provide the optimum total value in terms of return on investment and compliance with customer-centered accuracy, defect, and/or service levels.

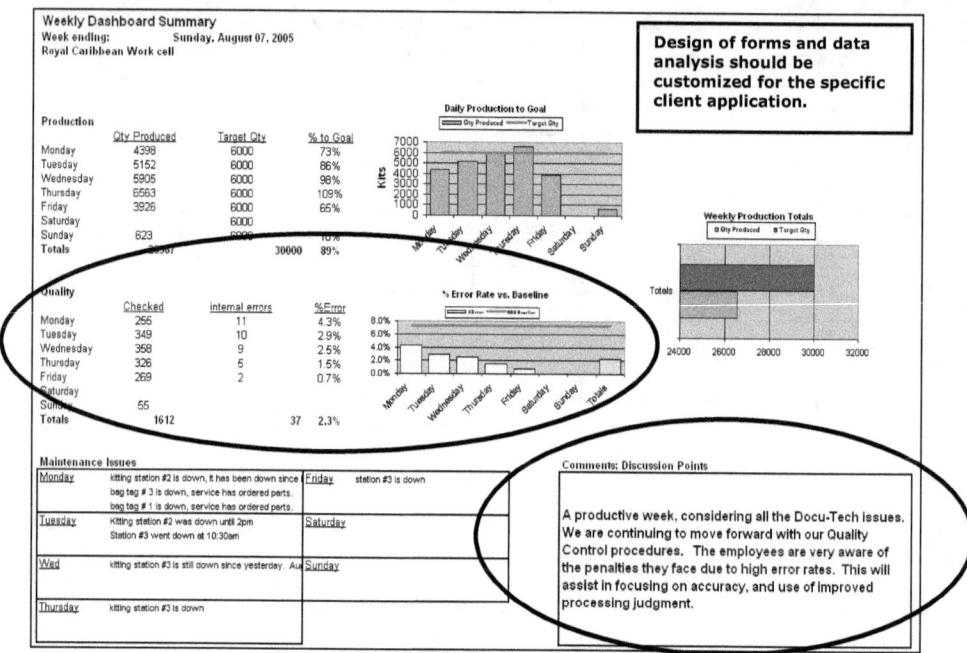

With this information in hand, corrective actions and process capability improvement initiatives may be best focused toward achievement of customer-centered quality conformance relative to product accuracy and service level attainment. At the end of the day, we must all keep well in mind what Mr. Bryan Joyner, author of the publication *Quality Excellence* stated, "Quality is what the customer says it is." We must define and quantify customer requirements and expectations. We must then measure, compile, track, and analyze our total performance against those targets in order to factually know where we are, as well as in which direction we are moving in relation to consistently meeting requirements and expectations of our customers, as well as effectively manage efficiencies, contain total costs, and advance financial performance.

c. Validation of Raw Materials:

Just as the old saying goes, "You can't make good chicken salad out of just feet and feathers." Consistently conforming products and on-time delivery performance cannot be effectively achieved with inconsistent and/or inferior raw materials and components. Through the focused efforts of our materials coordinators, leads, supervisors, auditing, and on-site management personnel, the following can readily be determined:

- Do the items staged for a specific production order match the item numbers as specified on the corresponding product bill of materials (BOM) or work instructions package?
- Do the items internal to the carton correspond to the external identification as labeled on the carton?
- Does the color, shape, size, consistency, etc. meet with previously supplied similar and/or the same items?
- Do the quantities staged correspond with the completed finished product quantities as specified within the work instructions or production order information?
- Are there any other irregularities and/or inconsistencies that require management and/or customer attention?

Any and all questions and/or concerns surfaced must be resolved with the customer's involvement prior to introduction of the materials and/or components into the assembly process. The pallet ID labeling and/or the production order document may then be initialed by the appropriate materials coordinator, auditor, and/or supervisor as confirmed prior to production start. Effective data collection in regard to materials and component irregularities must be captured and analyzed as part of the overall and comprehensive in-process quality data management regimen.

There are perhaps times where the tyranny of the urgent pushes aside the value of the important. In other words, decisions are sometimes made thinking that the specific product or order may be started and as the non-conforming materials or shortages are resolved, time and cost will somehow be saved and the customer's requirements best met. Please consider:

- Established methods or process may be altered impacting efficiencies (added labor cost),
- Production flows will be interrupted, products and materials moved off-line (added labor cost),

- Product flows will need to be re-started thereby impacting efficiencies, products and materials moved back into line (added labor cost),
- Increased opportunity for product contamination and/or damage (added materials cost / product losses / bill-back charges),
- As the production process is started, Staffmark / Output Solutions shares ownership and accountability for materials and components over which we have little if any direct impact or direct control (added management costs).

These added costs must be recognized and production orders held in pending status until raw materials and components are validated as accurate, conforming, and complete. Only then, may the production order be most cost-effectively introduced into the production process.

Thorough in-bound observation and management relative to total conformance of raw materials and components, in conjunction with appropriate corrective actions in regard to those observations, will contribute significantly to advancement of overall efficiencies, maintenance of cost controls, and enhancement of total financial performance.

d. Validation of Specifications, Work Instructions, and Samples:

"Excellence is never an accident."

Anonymous

The only possible way to avoid the development and communication of clear, concise, complete, and thorough product specifications, work instructions, and actual finished produst samples is to only hire physics into the work force. That way they will already know everything that is expected by the customer. If we are not in 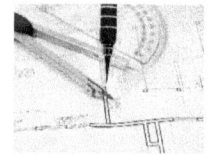 position to do that, then communication of these detailed instructions, specifications, and requirements must be effectively delivered and dispersed to an increasing language-diverse group.

In addition, as instructions, specifications, and/or samples are incomplete and/or inaccurate, it is highly unlikely that a consistent, accurate, and fully conforming product and/or service will be delivered, much less on time, everytime.

Here again, the materials coordinator, lead, auditing, and/or supervisory functions must validate as correct, complete, and accurate, any and all work instructions, specifications, and/or samples prior to the start of actual in-line production. In addition, it is incumbent upon on-site management and/or their designate to work with the client / customer to correct and resolve any inconsistencies or discrepencies. The daily / shift production worksheet (DPW) provides an excellent vehicle to facilitate consistent validation and confirmation of specifications, work instructions, and samples.

Design of forms and data analysis should be customized for the specific application.

SHIFT PRODUCTION WORKSHEET BY JOB			LINE LEAD:					
DATE:			CUST:					
SHIFT:			DESCRIPTION					
			JOB #		Standard per H			
EMPLOYEES					Pre Job Check List		Yes	No
NAME		START TIME:	END TIME:	HOURS WORKED	Work Instructions Received and Understood			
					QC Sample approved and reviewed			
1					Raw Materials Audited to the BOM and matches the skid ticket			
2					Understood amount due for the shift and assigned appropriate number of personnel based upon the standard			
3								
4					Work space is properly set up			
5					Post Shift Check List		Yes	No
6					DPW is legible and 100% accurate			
7					Work area is completely clean			
8					All finished product is accounted			
9					All raw material is counted and organized neatly on skids			
10					Quality			
11					Time	Quantity QCed	Defects	Defect Descriptions
12								
13								
14								
15								
16								
17								
18					I have reviewed each defect with the individual(s) responsible and corrected in real time. I have insured we are delivering a high quality product.		Y	N
19								
20					Completed Bindery Ticket Log			
21					Job #	Customer	Tckt No.	Received By
22					1			
23					2			
24					3			
25					4			
TOTAL MAN HOURS					5			
STANDARD X TOTAL MAN HOURS					6			
EFFICIENCY = Total Produced/(Standard X Total Man Hours)					7			
Comments:					8			
					9			
					10			
						Total Produced		

The pre-job check list must be completed by the responsible lead or supervisory personnel and then should be re-confirmed and initialed by the designated in-process auditor or alternate lead or supervisor, prior to the start of any work activity. Here again, the most inefficient and costly manner in which to manufacture any product or deliver any service is to do it once and then over again due to needed correction due to erroneous, incomplete, or misunderstood instructions or other processing information. Clear, concise, and well understood product information is as vital to effective cost control, efficiency management, and financial performance as any other process input, material or otherwise.

e. **Confirmation of Line and Work Place Configurations:**

"The beacons of productivity and innovation must be our guideposts. If we continue to _improve productivity of all key resources_ and our innovative standing, we are going to be profitable."

Peter Drucker, "Managing for the Future"

What is our most important, valuable, and costly resource? It is our labor resource. We must effectively and efficiently organize work at the individual level in order to best utilize this most costly of all key resources.

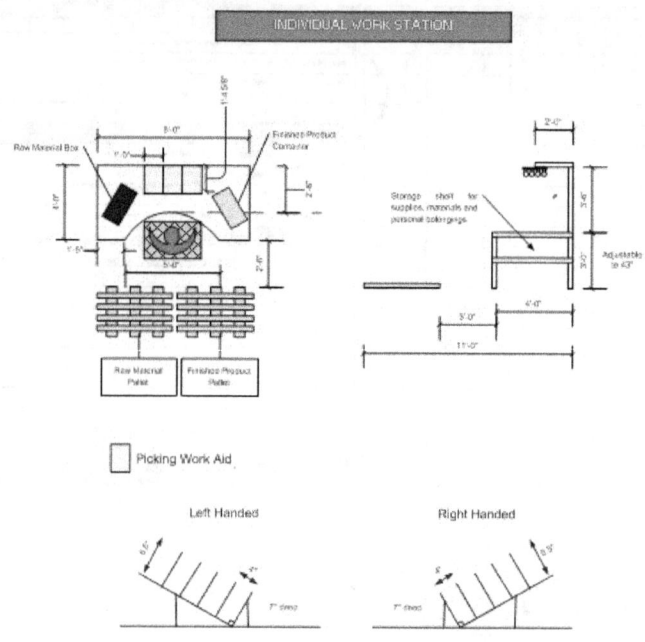

Work must be organized, components and materials must be positioned and arrayed in order to provide even the least experienced individual within the work force the maximum opportunity for efficiency of motion and most importantly, _operational accuracy._ Here again, the most efficient way to perform any task is "right the first time." It is the responsibility of management, engineering, and supervision to assure that our production associates have the greatest opportunity to perform their individual tasks safely, efficiently, and most importantly, _correctly._

Please note in the above illustration, there is a standard pattern for the positioning of materials and components in the prescribed order of assembly. The orientation of each material and/or component must correspond to that within the final assembled product. The materials and components are arrayed in an arch configuration to facilitate ease of reach and movement. The work area is adequately lighted. Numerous studies have demonstrated a direct correlation with lighting levels and accuracy of work performed. In addition, an anti-fatigue mat is in place for the associate. Fatigue and/or discomfort in the feet, ankles, knees, and legs indeed robs focused concentration from the accuracy of the work at hand, especially toward the later hours of the work day.

B	LINE LEAD:							
	CUST:							
	DESCRIPTION							
	JOB #			Standard per Hour				
			Pre Job Check List				Yes	No
RT TIME:	END TIME:	HOURS WORKED	Work Instructions Received and Understood					
			QC Sample approved and reviewed					
			Raw Materials Audited to the BOM and matches the skid ticket					
			Understand amount due for the shift and assigned appropriate number of personnel based upon the standard					
			Work space is properly set up					
			Post Shift Check List				Yes	No
			DPW is legible and 100% accurate					
			Work area is completely clean					
			All finished product is accounted					
			All raw material is counted and organized neatly on skids					
			Quality					
			Time	Quanitity QCed		Defects	Defect Descriptions	

Design of forms and data collection should be customized for the specific application.

Please note that on the shift / daily production work sheet (DPW) that a confirmation / validation is required in regard to proper configuration of the work area.

Please note that sitting is not necessarily an ergonomically sound option to standing as pressures and rotations are shifted to the back, hips, and shoulders. Reach and overall movement are reduced. Facilitation of the associate's movement into other adjacent work areas is significantly diminished. In addition, there is the cost of the production seating as well as the added space the chairs consume.

One of our primary work areas as managers, engineers, supervisors, and leads is to provide the maximum opportunity, relative to the set up and configuration of the work place, for each and every one of our most valuable resources, our associates, to achieve individual success. As our associates are productive and highly accurate in their outputs, we in turn, have maximized our opportunity for greater overall efficiencies, improved control of labor costs, and enhanced total financial performance.

"The harder you work the luckier you get."

Gary Player

f. Work-In-Process Audit / Validation of Assembly Conformance:

"You can observe a lot just by watching."

Yogi Berra

Don't we all focus with greater concentration upon the work at hand when we know that someone is going to periodically and unpredictably come by, carefully inspect our outputs, record their finding in detail, summarize those findings, and report on the accuracy of our performance to our superiors. You bet we do!

That is the perhaps the most impactful aspect of effective in-process sampling. It is the positive physiological impact upon the work force in regard to maintaining their collective mental focus upon achieving the required output accuracy parameters for the work being performed. This may well be achieved through the consistent in-process sampling efforts of a dedicated in-process auditor, line lead, and/or supervisor. The key element is that it is properly and thoroughly accomplished. This is by no means a new innovation. This is perhaps the single oldest and most effective quality process control technique. That is having a designated individual in an appropriate position of authority carefully examining outputs at the individual level and associating that individuals name with their findings. This, in turn, should have a significant impact upon that specific individual's job security, either positive or negative. In-process sampling will also have a profound effect upon that specific individual's efficiency and total earnings capability as lots or batches (cartons, totes, pallets, etc. – whatever is applicable to that specific processing situation) are rejected back to the responsible production associate for 100% re-inspection and correction of any non-conformances.

In-Process Audit Data Collection Worksheet:

AUDITOR: _____ CUSTOMER: _____

SUPERVISOR: _____ MANAGER: _____

Design of forms and data collection should be customized for the specific application.

#	Associate:	# Units Inspected:	# Errors:	Error Type(s):	Time:	Date:	Shift:	Line:	Operation:	Product:	COMMENTS:
1					:						
2					:						
3					:						
4					:						
5					:						
6					:						
7					:						
8					:						
9					:						
10					:						

This in-process rejection, re-inspection, immediate corrective action, and documentation in regard to all non-conformances surfaced in-process is the cornerstone of any effective quality assurance program. It is just like a house rule that many of our mothers strictly enforced, "If you break it – you fix it . . . if you messed it up – you clean it up!" This most fundamental and basic level of associate accountability is absolutely vital to an effective and sustainable quality process control system.

In addition, if all inspection is performed at end-of-line or only as end-item audits, then it is often too late and far more expensive. The re-inspection and correction costs may be substantially higher as well as possibly destructive in regard to product function and/or integrity. Also, end-of-process inspection may also result in hundreds, thousands, or possibly tens of thousands of units being produced or processed before the non-conformance is discovered. This situation will be *extremely* costly!

"Quality goes up when management has high expectations for their staff."

From "Commitment to Quality"

The non-conformance data collected, assimilated, and analyzed from real-time sampling will also provide an excellent platform from which corrective actions may be formulated and launched and cost-effective continuous improvement initiatives established and maintained. Additionally, the conformance data collected, assimilated, and analyzed from this real-time sampling may also provide an excellent platform from which to initiate individual and group recognition and rewards programs that reinforce positive, desired quality related behaviors and achievements.

"If anything goes real good, then the players did it. That's all it takes to get people to win football games."

Paul "Bear" Bryant

While there is an investment in manpower and administrative cost in regard to thorough and detailed in-process sampling, data collection, assimilation, and analysis, this may well be the single most valuable and effective of all quality management tools. As Mr. Berra so well stated that we can observe a lot if we will just 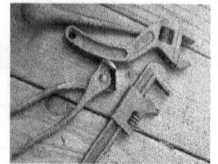 watch! Here again, as our individual associates are productive and highly accurate in their outputs, we in turn, will maximize our opportunity for greater overall efficiencies, improved control of total costs, and enhanced overall financial performance.

g. End-Item Audit Validation of Packaging, Labeling, and Skidding Conformance:

"Some people make things happen, others let things happen, and some . . . wonder what happened!"

Anonymous

When it comes to process accuracy, conformance to customer requirements, and on-time delivery of products and services, do we want to find ourselves wondering what happened! That is by no means the way to maximize our potential for success, customer satisfaction, and financial performance excellence. Yet this is so often the case  that we discover from the client, or worse yet, the end purchaser or consumer that our delivery, quality, and/or accuracy performance as it relates to fully conforming to requirements fell short and we have a very dissatisfied client and a most unhappy product purchaser and/or end user.

The packing associate, materials coordinator, in-process auditor, line lead, and/or supervisor may be well positioned to perform this final validation of product or service conformance prior to the final hand-off to our client company. This consists of verification via sampling and confirmation of:

    viii. Final assembly,
    ix. Packaging,
    x. Shipping carton type / size,
    xi. Carton counts,
    xii. Product and/or carton labeling,

xiii. Pallet type / size,

xiv. Pallet carton counts,

xv. Pallet wrapping configuration,

xvi. Pallet labeling,

xvii. Appropriate staging for client pick-up.

This is typically referred to as the end-item audit as now conformance to all product assembly, packaging, labeling, palletizing, and shipping requirements may be validated and confirmed. The In-Process Audit Data Collection Worksheet will function as an effective data collection and assimilation vehicle.

In-Process Audit Data Collection Worksheet:

| AUDITOR: _____ | CUSTOMER: _____ |
| SUPERVISOR: _____ | MANAGER: _____ |

> Design of forms and data collection should be customized for the specific client application.

#	Associate:	# Units Inspected:	# Errors:	Error Type(s):	Time:	Date:	Shift:	Line:	Operation:	Product:	COMMENTS:
1				:							
2				:							
3				:							
4				:							
5				:							
6				:							

Here again, excellence is not an accident and the harder we work the luckier we get! Capable management must make it happen! Final validation of our product and service conformance to all customer requirements is a most critical element to achieving greater overall efficiencies, improved control of total costs, and enhanced overall financial performance.

h. Corrective Action Management:

"If you make a mistake, a real faux pas, you should: Admit it. Apologize if you've offended. Take responsibility for it. Don't try to hide it. Don't try to make excuses. Don't do it again!"

Lodwrick Cook, Chairman and CEO, Arco
Taken from "Lions Don't Need to Roar"

We all naturally want to do the right things. What's right for your customer? What's right for your company? What's right for our people? What's right for us? This is often a complex equation to resolve. Abdication, denial, and no action at all are the worst things you can do. Yet, many factors and variables come into play:

- The number of actionable opportunities,
- The criteria used for taking corrective actions,
- The involvement and input of other stakeholders in the corrective action process,
- The reactions to and effects of those corrective actions.

There is a structured and systematic process, a specific and effective methodology that can be utilized when formulating deploying corrective actions. The key factors of an effective corrective actions structure should encompass the following areas:

1. **Identify the Goal or End Result You Wish to Achieve:**

    Who is the customer? What are their needs, requirements, and concerns? What do we want to accomplish and ultimately achieve? What is the goal? Also consider and evaluate, how much time do you have in order to make the best decision practical? When do you need to act? You should be proactive and get the information you need. It is often good to slow things down. You usually have more time than you initially think that you do. Negotiate if you think more time is needed in order for you to formulate solid corrective actions. What is to be gained by delivering a decision before it is needed? What is to be gained by investing the time to fully evaluate the issues, explore options and alternatives, solicit input from other involved or informed sources, and trial test pre-selected options? A great deal!

2. **Identify Who Will Be Involved in the Implementation or Who Has a Vested Interest in the Outcome:**

    Ask yourself, from among all the stakeholders, who should be a part of the corrective action team and/or included within the team member structure? Determine what specialized expertise, not already on the corrective action team, you may need to include as a part of the total team. Is financial, legal, human resource, engineering, mechanical, sales, marketing, systems, etc. expertise required in order to make a sound decision?

3. **With the Decision Making Team in Place, Reconfirm and Redefine the Goal or Results That Are to Be Achieved**

Reconfirm, who is the customer? What are their needs & concerns? What must be accomplished, ultimately achieved? What is the goal?

With this corrective action team structure in place and utilized, poor or inappropriate decisions become harder to make. These individuals on your decision making team, as your partners and team members, also want what's in the customer's, organization's, employee's, and your collective long-term best interests. All must recognize that success is mutual and long-term. Everyone must think win-win.

Your corrective action team structure is in place. Your customer-centered goals and results are clearly defined. One of the best guides for effective corrective actions management is the traditional and time-proven *5-Step Problem Solving Process.*

1. **Investigate and Define the Issues:**
   a. Clearly describe the problem,
   b. Listen to and understand all sides,
   c. Focus on data and measurement,
   d. Specify items and issues, not blame,
   e. Determine scope or size of the issue,
   f. Quantify the goal(s), the result to be achieved,
   g. Determine the measure of completion.
   (How and when will you know it's corrected? This could be percentage of improvement from a baseline, a selected numerical target, an indices, etc.)
   h. Target the resolution date.

2. **Fix (Temporarily) the Problem:**
   a. Temporarily patch the process to keep going,
   b. Protect customers and employees,
   c. This solution is not to be totally cost effective. It is not a permanent solution.

3. **Identify the Root Cause(s):**
   a. Chart or map the dysfunctional process,
   b. Review all customer needs and requirements,
   c. Look for threads of similarity / commonality,
   d. Look for opportunity for mishap,
   e. Construct a cause and effect diagram,
   f. Develop a Praeto (80% / 20% rule) analysis.

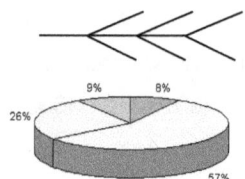

Root Cause Analysis: Master						
KITTING							
Error Date: 092006, 092106	Item Number: TAPP BINDER	Order Number: 95187090, 25012 016, 15646818, 51317431, 96071 936,	External -		Internal - Wrong orientation, dirty and/or damaged documents	Responsible Resources: Kitting Dept.
			Closed Date:			Personnel Completing Root Cause Analysis: George Singerline
Error Keyword: Errors on TAPP Binders							
Error Description: General Description Tabs in Right placement but inserted in binder with wrong orientation. Documents in binder in protective sleeve but orientated wrong. Dirty, damaged or marked documents used. Protective sleeve torn. Specific details							
CORRECTIVE ACTION No Charge for these Projects Loss of incentive pay and disciplinary action for those involved.							
Root Cause of Error: A break down of QC process, 100% of QCs were not conducted properly. Personnel involved: staffmark shift supervision, leads, and production workers. Moore Wallace kitting coordinators.							
Preventative Action: Tighter QC process. Re-Train on 100% QC SOP with appropriate leads, (Request assistance from Moore Wallace to re-train leads on QC SOP in no later than the next 5 business days to ensure proper QC specifications are met) Make sure em							

I understand the importance of accurately reporting issues requiring Root Cause Analysis and I confirm that the information listed above accurately represents what actually occurred the date in question.

_____   _____
Insert Name   Insert Name

The format above has proven to be an excellent tool relative to determination of root caused and providing the platform for focused, concerted corrective actions.

4. **Take Constructive / Corrective Action:**
   a. Generate all possible solutions,
   b. Evaluate and select the most practical solution,
   c. Identify least complexity and cost,

d. Identify least time requirement,
e. Identify which solution provides best prevention,
f. Determine which solution is the most implementable,
g. Plan, document, and communicate implementation,
h. Implement corrective action plan,
i. Document, track, and communicate implementation performance.

5. Evaluate and Follow Up:
a. Appraise effectiveness of your implementation relative to the predetermined measure of completion,
b. Follow-up through:
   i. Audits,
   ii. Surveys,
   iii. Informal communication, meetings, reviews, feedback questions.

To establish and maintain an effective corrective action process and structure first identify the goal(s) or results you wish to achieve. Next, determine how much time you have in order to make the best decision practical. Next, identify who will be involved in the corrective action implementation and who has a vested interest in the outcome. Next, determine what specialized expertise, not already on the corrective action team, that may be needed as a part of the team. With the corrective action team in place, reconfirm and / or redefine the goal(s) or results you wish to achieve. Now you should proceed with the 5-step corrective action process of, 1) investigate and define the issues, 2) fix (temporarily) the problem, 3) identify the root cause(s), 4) take focused corrective action, and 5) evaluate and follow up.

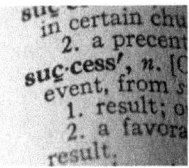

Your ability to effectively implement timely and effective corrective actions, with the support of your people, partners, and customers, is a most critical managerial skill that will greatly enhance the opportunities for improved control of total costs, and enhanced overall financial performance.

I. Data Analysis and Reporting:

"What gets measured . . . gets done."

Peter Drucker

Within the fundamental framework of quality assurance manage resides the aspects of measurement, analysis, and reporting. For example, would we drive a car with no speedometer, fuel gauge, or odometer? It would hardly be sound transportation management if we addressed our fuel needs only when we ran out of gas along the side of the road! Yet is this not how many managers attempt to run their business?

We must know how our processes and the individuals within them are performing in regard to consistency and accuracy relative to meeting customer requirements and service parameters. We must have accurate and concise information to know both where we currently are, as well as in what direction we are going. We must measure and communicate those measurements.

One of the most useful and cost effective tools available is the standard Excel spreadsheet, in conjunction with its analysis and charting capabilities. Data may be assimilated, analyzed, tracked, and charted on a daily, weekly, monthly, and quarterly basis. This format, in conjunction with the entire weekly performance dashboard, also provides an excellent vehicle to also communicate performance information to the client's internal management as well as to the upper management of Staffmark / Output Solutions.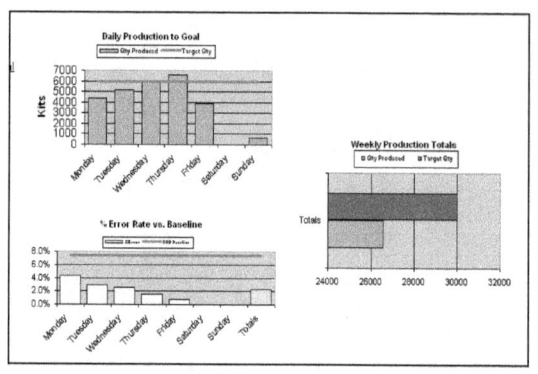

The establishment and maintenance of these reporting vehicles and structures may also be compared to keeping score for the game. How long would any athletic event hold our interest if we had no idea who was winning, who was losing, or what winning even looked like? The measurements verses targets can be used in three very effective ways. The first, as performance is visually communicated that is below the established target or goal, cognitive dissonance, is created. That is that somewhat uncomfortable feeling inside when you know that a key aspect of your work quality, results accuracy, and levels of service are falling short of meeting requirements and expectations.

What happens when that accuracy or service level goal or target is ultimately achieved? That dissonance is replaced with a positive internal reaction of satisfaction and achievement. Again, for this to happen, measurements must be compiled, tracked, compared to goals, and visually communicated to all stakeholders.

The second, as accuracy and service level targets and goals are achieved and surpassed, we as managers set our work team to win! As we win, we can then recognize, reward, and celebrate our achievements! Everyone wants to be associated with a 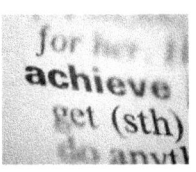 winning team. Capable managers set their teams up to achieve, succeed, and win, then reward and recognize the team's quality, accuracy, and service level accomplishments.

"There are two things that people want more than money and sex . . . **recognition and praise.**"

Mary Kay Ash

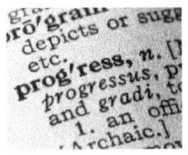 We must recognize quality, service, and accuracy progress, notable achievement, and goal attainment. We should, according to Ken Blanchard, "Catch our people doing things right!" Make this an integral part of your daily management routine. Generously, specifically, and sincerely praise progress, notable achievement, and incremental goal attainment. Celebrate successes by investing generously in morale and team building activities. Increase the *fun factor*! Things that get rewarded get done, so establish rewards that reinforce the attitudes, behaviors, and accomplishments that maximize our opportunities for greater overall efficiencies, increased output accuracy and delivery reliability, improved control of total costs, and enhanced overall financial performance.

Staffing
Calculation
Level
Projection

2. Staffing Calculation Level Projection:

a. Client Partnership and Communication:

We might define partnership as a relationship between individuals and groups that is characterized by mutual cooperation and responsibility, as for the achievement of a specified goal. In order to maximize your opportunities for  managerial and leadership success, you must develop and maintain collaborative partnerships with those individuals who have a vested interest in the achievement of our goals and objectives. These individuals can be both internal as well as external to the organization.

You must recognize that in order for you to be totally successful, you must collaboratively incorporate all the brain power, the expertise, within a collective functional group, as you together focus upon achievement of your mutual goals. While some may suggest that this is just good teamwork and they would be basically correct, a partnership is inclusive of teamwork, yet it embraces some different aspects.

These individuals from these other functional disciplines are essentially our peers, and in some instances, our superiors. Primary goals and objectives are mutually shared. Your roles and responsibilities are mutually understood, yet differ, and yet are fully compatible and collaborative. You and your partner are strongly interdependent. You heavily depend upon each other for success and share in that mutual success.

Collective expertise is pooled and shared for mutual benefit. Your relationship is continuous and long-term. You often share the same end customer / consumer. You need each other to succeed. A negative relationship with our functional partners can be a great disability to your ongoing success, possibly even professionally terminal.

These partners can come from within other functional areas of the organization. However, they can come from outside. Suppliers, vendors, contractors, consultants, customers, you mutually cooperate, collaborate, and pool your collective expertise toward the achievement of a shared goal. You mutually depend upon each other to succeed. Your interdependence better assures your mutual, ongoing, and long-term success.

How do you establish and maintain these partnerships with our client? It can be accomplished through the application of your interpersonal skills. In a conducive meeting / communication environment ask variations on those key managerial and leadership performance questions:

- What are the things that we together must accomplish to be successful?
- How can we together provide better products & support to our mutual customers?
- How can we together be mutually successful long-term?

W. Edwards Deming's philosophy is to establish long-term relationships with suppliers / vendors based upon trust and mutual benefit, not just price, but long-term total cost. We should be thinking win - win - win. If the client / customer wins - and your functional / supplier partners win - you all win.

Your ability to develop and maintain collaborative partnerships with those individuals within our client's organization who have a vested interest in the achievement of your goals and objectives is another critical managerial and leadership skill that is essential to unleashing the power of the workforce on the path to success.

"Satisfied customers are the most important asset of any business. Our mission is to understand their needs, values, fears, and goals. We must learn to see through their eyes. If we serve customers with creativity, compassion, and competence . . . the competition may catch on . . . but they will never catch up."

Anonymous

b. Partnership, Support, and Communication:

"I not only use all the brains I have, but all I can borrow."

Woodrow Wilson

No manager of any operation is an island unto themselves. Regardless of one's background and experience, a plethora of technical skills must be concertedly and effectively focused on key results attainment. A successful operation must be supported with:

- Area / job advertising,
- Recruiting,
- Application processing,
- Applicant interviewing / screening,
- Background validation,
- Hiring,
- Orientation,
- Gross-to-net payroll,
- Benefits administration,
- Client relationship management.

This range of functional support must all be provided and/or supported by, with, and through the local branch and regional offices. Without them and their critical support across this broad spectrum of human resource management needs and requirements, in conjunction with customer relationship support, who alone con succeed?

It is also critical that we as operational, on-site managers take a leadership role in communicating with and thoroughly involving the local branch office and involving them to the fullest extent possible in the development and continuing maintenance of superlative total account performance and relationship management.

As on-site, operational mangers, you have a tremendous load of responsibility and accountability in regard to total performance delivery. You cannot accomplish this challenging task alone. There are no successful "Lone Rangers" in today's demanding and complex operational environments. Branch partnership, support, and communication are critical elements for success!

"We may have come on different ships, but we are all in the same boat now."

Dr. Martin Luther King

c. Projection of Weekly Volume Forecast:

"It is just as if you are blindfolded and cannot hit a target that you cannot see . . . you likewise cannot hit a target that you do not have!"

Zig Ziglar

What job did we have that it wasn't important what we got accomplished by the end of the day and/or the end of the week? I know that I have never had a job like that. Every job that I have ever performed had performance and delivery requirements attached to it. My Dad would tell me, "Get that wagon load of wood cut and stacked before supper." It was clear as to how much was expected and by when. The reward was also clear . . . I got to eat (and keep warm!).

All clients and customers want and need the delivery of products and/or services within specific timeframes and at specified volume levels. A solid partnership in conjunction with strong communication lines is critical. Sharing of annual, quarterly, weekly, and daily production volumes, targets, and goals is absolutely vital to success. This information, irrespective of total accuracy, must be available to directionally plan for and allocate manpower and resources.

Often, concerns in regard to accuracy surface. However, that is just a real world situation. Out at 90 days, a production volume forecast may have a +/- 40% window accuracy. That is better that knowing nothing! Out at 30 days, an updated / revised production volume forecast may have a +/- 20% window of accuracy. That is still far better than knowing nothing! Out at 15 days, an updated / revised production volume forecast may have a +/- 10% window of accuracy. Still . . . a great deal better than knowing nothing. Out at 7 days, an updated / revised production volume forecast may have a +/- 5% window of accuracy. That is well within normal operational tolerances for many environments. The key is that as we move down the forecast-

time continuum, we initially have a general direction that narrows, focuses, and improves relative to accuracy as we move down the continuum. Variables are reduced in conjunction with updated customer / market information being made available. This may be compared to a funnel that is wide and open at the top;

however, it narrows and focuses as we move down the funnel into a narrowed opening at the bottom.

The key again is that this production volume forecasting and updating is appropriately shared with us as an operating partner with mutual, shared accountability for the attainment of production volume targets. This level of communication and proprietary information sharing rarely just spontaneously occurs. It must be initiated, nurtured, supported, and maintained through the proactive efforts of skilled on-site management.

With a general, directional volume forecast available, general, directional resource allocation and planning may ensue. Those plans are updated, adjusted, and refined with each new and improving forecast. With a reasonably accurate production forecasts available, final staffing plans and human resource allocation may be totally developed and fully deployed in order to meet the projected demand. However, there will always and forever be un-forecasted demand, rush orders, materials delivery delays, last minute specification updates, machine downtime issues, and numerous other unforeseen and un-forecast-able events and occurrences that will require daily, and sometimes hourly adjustments in actual production and resource allocation plans and initiatives.

Forecasts are subject to constant and unending revision. Extended forecasts begin with a wide variance of accuracy and improve as time frames move in. Likewise human resource allocation must move, modify, and adjust with revised / updated forecasting. And always remember, any forecast is preferable to no forecast, and any planning is preferable to no planning and just simply reacting!

d. Definition / Identification of Daily Production Volume Requirements:

"How do you eat an elephant . . . .? One bite at a time!"

Now that our production volume forecast has been developed and communicated, we know what the week and hopefully the weeks ahead look like. Let's say for example our production schedule requires the completion of 1,000,000 units for the week. We have 50

work stations available. We also have facility availability up to three shifts. However, we also must consider that we *will* encounter absenteeism, turnover, machine downtime, and materials flow interruption. We also must remember that the most expensive way to do anything is on overtime. Therefore, we should base our actual operating schedule on a 35 to 36 actual working hour week. Therefore, as these above factors impact upon our volume capability, actual average working hours will be pushed up toward 40 (37, 38, 39 . . . .) - not over 40 (41, 42, 43 . . .) and into overtime premium costs.

The production equation should be as follows: 1,000,000 units per week / 3 shifts = 333,333 units per shift-week / 35 weekly shift hours = 9,524 units per shift hour / 50 production associates per shift = 190 completed units per production associate per hour / 60 minutes per hour = 3.2 completed units per production associate per minute (or 1 completed unit per 18.8 seconds). Completing 1 unit every 18.8 seconds X 50 associates X 35 work hours X 3 shifts = 1.0+M completed units doesn't sound nearly as intimidating! We can also establish a test model to confirm that 18.8 seconds is a realistic time allowance for unit completion.

With this target clearly defined, we can establish hourly, daily, shift, and weekly production volume performance goals at the individual, team, line, area, shift, or any other level deemed appropriate relative to producing and reliably delivering our production volume requirements. By tracking and visually posting actual output performance, if actual results fall below required targets, then appropriate corrective action measures can be developed and deployed.

In addition, as these production performance goals are visually established and actual hourly and daily results are tracked and visually posted and compared to targets, we have established a process whereby achievement can be recognized and rewarded and our organization set up to win!

e. Projection of Efficiencies:

"You people will generally perform up to, or down to, management's demonstrated level of expectations."

Why expect and/or tolerate less than 100% performance from every trained member of the production team? Let's perform the old card dealing exercise. Holding the deck stationary in front of you, deal the cards into four stacks at the corners of a 12" square at the rate of one (1) card per second. As you can  both see and feel, this is a reasonably sustainable pace. It can well be comfortably sustainable for a full shift. Achieving the required quality requirements is straightforward and realistically attainable. A safe environment is also well maintained.

All production standards are based upon this fundamental premise. A trained individual can comfortably and safely maintain a consistent pace, with appropriate rest periods, for the period of a full shift. Integral to this approach, is also the opportunity for the trained associate to achieve performance levels, well above 100%, without compromising quality and/or safety.

However, there are situations wherein rising the performance bar up to 120% may be considered.
- The production group or team is highly skilled and experienced associates.
- The product has a high degree of familiarity.
- The product has a straightforward, less complex construction.
- A combination of any or all or the above.

Likewise, there are situations wherein lowering the performance bar down to 80% may be considered.
- The production group or team is inexperienced, newly trained associates.
- The product has a high degree of complexity.
- The product has little familiarity.
- A combination of any or all or the above.

Admittedly, this may be, at times a somewhat subjective process initially. It is also highly recommended that the responsible manager solicit the input of the production supervisors and/or production leads that may be involved with the start-up and ongoing production of the specific product and or production group under consideration. Their buy-in and process ownership is essential.

The key objective of this approach is two-fold. As a production manager, we must assure an adequate and consistent supply of products and materials in order to allow the respective production line and/or unit to achieve its full capability and thereby provide an adequate level of earnings potential for the corresponding production associate group. Also, as a production manager, we must fully provide for 100% completion of our committed production output. Our client must be in position to 100% rely upon our production volume commitment. We must deliver on time, every time.

We must never forget our foundational mission . . .

"Deliver on time, with quality excellence, at the lowest possible total cost."

If this mission cannot be consistently achieved, in the above order, then our replacements will have the opportunity to do so! Establishing appropriate production targets, with the appropriate level of efficiency to be achieved, and demonstrating full confidence in their attainment, is one of the cornerstones of production management success.

f. S.A.M.'s / Production Standards Definition:

Standard Allowed Minutes (S.A.M.'s) are the most basic of all labor measurement building blocks. We must know within a reasonable range of accuracy, how much actual labor / work is required per unit at 100% efficiency in order to effectively projects costs, direct and indirect (supervisors, leads, materials coordinators, QA staff, and administrative support) staffing levels, equipment needs, floor layout, space requirements, quality requirements, and on-time delivery schedules. That's about it!

60 Minutes / S.A.M.'s Per Unit = Required Production Level per Person per Hour @ 100%

While there are a number of accurate and well accepted approaches to work measurement (time study, MTM, MOST, GSD), none are any more effective that the engineering analyst's understanding of the products, environment, quality requirements, and total application. In my view, actual time study encompassing full interaction with and observations of the total environment and the production associates within it, in conjunction with its inherent requirements, obstacles, delays, and other parameters provide a far more thorough approach for the time study / engineering analyst.

No other approach gains the confidence of the production group which includes production supervision and management. Without their full confidence in and complete support of any standards developed and deployed, effective achievement of those standards is severely compromised. The support of all levels of production management relative to their confidence level in the fairness, accuracy, and achieve-ability of the production standard is one of the single most critical elements to engineering success.

Once a thorough and complete time study battery has been compiled and corresponding production time data and standards developed, these in turn, can provide the basis for a standard data menu of work components. These can then be appropriately applied with appropriate levels of accuracy and confidence. However, these standards developed from this historical, standard data would require that they be confirmed and/or adjusted via a thorough time study.

As mentioned, MTM, MOST, GSD, and other predetermined data systems and approached can be applied with high levels of accuracy provided the analyst has a thorough understanding of the product, quality standards, and total production environment. Here again, any standards developed and deployed require confirmation and/or adjustment via actual time study observation.

To again emphasize, the support of all levels of production management relative to their confidence level in the fairness, accuracy, and achieve-ability of the production standard is one of the single most critical elements to engineering success. This is ultimately best achieved through actual, in-depth, and thorough time study analysis.

g. Calculation of Staffing Projections:

Again, Standard Allowed Minutes are the most basic of all labor measurement building blocks. From a thorough, well identified, and detailed standard allowed minute per unit of measure, accuracy in development, control, and delivery of production volume requirements becomes far more predictive and deliverable. There are a number of approaches to production staffing and production volume capability development.

- ((Projected Weekly Production Volume / Available Weekly Production Hours) X Standard Allowed Minutes Per Unit) / 60 Minutes per Hour = Production Associates Required @ 100%. Projected associates required can then be divided by the anticipated efficiency to be achieved to yield the desired staffing levels.

    o 100,000 units needed / 36 available work hours = 2,778 completed units per hour needed X .750 S.A.M.'s per unit = 2,083 work minutes @ 100% required per hour / 60 minutes per work hour = 34.7 (round up to 35) production associates needed @ 100% to achieve the required output. If we were to project an efficiency of 80%, we would then need 43.4 (round up to 44) production associates. If we were to project 120% efficiency that would equate to 28.9 (round up to 29) production associates.

        - Note that the staffing differential between 44 associates at 80% verses 29 @ 120% would also have a financially positive impact upon total supervisory, training, materials coordination, QA, and administrative support needs.

Also note that 36 available production hours were utilized and not 40. First of all remember, the most expensive way to accomplish anything is on overtime. The following factors must be recognized and their impact upon available production hours must be taken into consideration.

- Absenteeism,
- Turnover,
- Machine downtime,
- Product change-over,
- Materials flow interruption,
- Materials conformance irregularities,
- Product rejection and re-work,

- Severe weather,

If 40 hours is factored into the production capability equation, then as the above events occur, and they **will** occur, then overtime $$$ is required in order to fulfill the production schedule commitment. However, in my experience, if a basis of 36 hours is utilized, then as these factors **do** occur, the production unit is not forced into an expensive overtime scenario in order to fulfill it on-time delivery commitments. Total staffing levels will be somewhat raised, however, the optimum economic balance is far better achieved and maintained with these production environment realities factored into the total production equation.

Of course then same basic logic path may be utilized from the standpoint of utilization of the available production capacity in place with the respective staffing level maintained as a constant.

- (Number of Available Production Associates X Available Weekly Production Hours X Efficiency % X 60 Minutes Per Hour) / (Standard Allowed Minutes Per Unit) = Projected Production Capacity Unit Volume

    - 35 Production Associates X 36 Available Hours X 100% Efficiency X 60 Minutes Per Hour = 75,600 Available Work Minutes / .750 S.A.M.'s Per Unit = 100,800 Projected Production Capacity Unit Volume

Let's suppose that within a given production week, fewer than anticipated volume capability impact factors have occurred. Therefore the following positive options exist:

- Pull in additional production volume from the period ahead if available.
- Utilize the production gains for an opportunity to pursue investment in production associate operational cross-training.
- Ask for volunteers to go home early (prior to end of shift and/or at week-end).
- Send the entire work force early (prior to end of shift and/or at week-end).
- Recognize and reward the work force for 100% on-time production schedule completion.

Our continuing mission is on-time production schedule completion, with quality excellence, at the lowest possible total cost. It is our sincerest desire that the concepts and tools presented above will support the delivery of excellence in on-time production schedule completion for our client companies, and in turn, their customers as well.

"If we don't serve the customer . . . someone else will!"

Anonymous

h. Communication of Needs:

Rarely do we plan to fail . . . we fail to plan. Planning, preparation, and communication of production capacity needs and requirements is critical. Open and effective communication with the client company's production scheduling management in regard to providing as much forward visibility is absolutely essential. With advance information, capacity plans can be formulated, associates can be recruited, hired, oriented and trained. Floor space, equipment, and work place needs can be identified and addressed.

Close communication with your supporting branch and human resource partners in regard to forward staffing needs is an absolutely critical element to achieving production schedule delivery success. Close communication with your industrial engineering partners is likewise critical relative to securing needed layouts, work flow, floor space requirements, work place needs, and equipment requirements is absolutely essential.

We must also consider the need to include within the communication process the entire production team as well. Management, supervision, leads, materials coordinators, administrative staff, and the production associates must all be stakeholders in the achievement of production schedule delivery excellence. It will take the fullest commitment and total concerted efforts of the entire production team in order to achieve production targets. We will all succeed (or all fail) together.

Please do not think for a moment that just hoping and wishing that somehow the production schedule will be miraculously achieved. It will not.

"Excellence is never and accident."

Anonymous

Production schedule performance excellence will not occur by accident. It requires a close client partnership, communication, and cooperation. It requires a close partnership, communication, and cooperation with human resource and engineering partners. It requires the full ownership and commitment of the entire production management, supervision, and support staff. It absolutely requires the fullest commitment and concerted efforts of the entire production staff.

Production Order Management

3. Production Order Management:

a. Client Communication and Order Prioritization:

"It is almost as important to know what is not serious as to know what is."

John Kenneth Gailbraith

Mr. Gailbraith makes an excellent point. We should be working on the most important and should not be working on the unimportant. This principle has solid application in the area of production order management. It is critical to effective delivery performance to be certain that we are working on the right things in the right order. It is so very important that we communicate closely with our clients and customers to be assured that we mutually have clear vision and insight into what is a priority . . . as well as to what is not a priority. Working in close partnership with our clients and customers, we must have production order requirements identified and categorized in appropriate priority order.

> To All Associates in the Work Pant & Jean Units:
>
> June 13, 2000
>
> In order to enhance our service and delivery to our customers we must improve our ability to finish cuts together and complete. In order to aid us in this initiative, beginning immediately, we are starting the "BRAVO" system. What that means is that all cuts loaded into line on *Monday* will be labeled with a *White* card. All cuts loaded into line on *Tuesday* will be labeled with a *Red* card. All cuts loaded into line on *Wednesday* will be labeled with a *Blue* card. All cuts loaded into line on *Thursday* will be labeled with a *Green* card. All cuts loaded into line on *Friday or Saturday* will be labeled with a *Gold* (yellow) card.
>
> All the *White* labeled bundles must be completed through your operation before beginning any *Red* labeled bundles. All *Red* labeled bundles must be completed through your operation before beginning any *Blue* labeled bundles. All *Blue* labeled bundles must be completed through your operation before beginning any *Green* labeled bundles. All *Green* labeled bundles must be completed through your operation before beginning any *Gold* (yellow) labeled bundles. All *Gold* labeled bundles must be completed through your operation before beginning any new *White* labeled bundles.
>
> If you have any questions or need additional assistance, please see your supervisor. We wish to thank each and every associate for their hard work and diligent efforts as we work together to meet our customers' demand for our high quality work apparel products.
>
> Production Manager: _____
> Production Engineer: _____
> Production Supervisor: _____
> Production Associate: _____

In any production system, output capability is not infinite. There are limitations and constraints with even the most robust of processes. Therefore, clear identification and production order classification within a priority sequence is a critical element to on-time delivery success.

This may be accomplished through the application of an alpha-numeric identification system, color coding, date sequencing, and/or a combination of methods. It is also imperative that floor management, supervision, materials coordination, as well as the production associates all are trained in, understand, and adhere to the production order prioritization system that is in place. Disciplined adherence to production order priority sequencing must be mandatory. Please note the above example of a color-date priority system deployed in a high-volume apparel manufacturing environment.

It is not as important what system of priority identification is utilized. The important factors are:

- Production orders are prioritized,
- An effective identification system is in place,
- The entire production staff understands it,
- The entire production staff strictly adheres to it.

b. Definition of Start / End Parameters:

"There is nothing so useless as doing efficiently that which should not be done at all."
Peter Drucker

Equally important in the production order management process is a clear definition and full understanding of all stakeholders as to where in the process is it our responsibility to begin, as well as at what point the final hand-off is to be made to the customer. We might refer to these as our **operational bookends**.

Does the process initiate with the supply trailer on the in-bound tarmac, with the supply trailer backed into the receiving dock, with the materials in the warehouse racking, or picked and staged into a queuing area? Who has responsibility for validation of materials and components delivered into the respective processing area? Are finished components palletized and delivered to a staging area? Are the completed products to be moved into warehousing racking and inventory? How has accountability for final quality assurance? Are finished products to be loaded onto out-bound trailers? Are trailers to be staged onto an out-bound tarmac? How area variances and discrepancies to be resolved? All these questions must be addressed and the appropriate processes structured and deployed in conjunction with accountability fully recognized and accepted. These areas must be fully encompassed within the frame work of a comprehensive operating agreement.

Not only is this critical from an effective operational standpoint, it is also imperative that these issues be clearly defined during the process of financial structuring as well. The actual production process – beginning to end – must accurately mirror the financial structure and modeling as well . . . and vice versa.

A highly efficient process may well be structured and in place, however, if functionality is being performed and delivered that falls outside the financial structure of the total program, money is being lost, no matter how efficiently it is being lost! We must assure that clear and concise agreement is reached and consistently maintained throughout the development, implementation, and continuing delivery of our products and services to our client companies.

c. Definition of On-Time Targets and Thru-Put Time:

"On to Little Big Horn for glory. We've caught them napping."

George A. Custer

Within the arena of effective production order management we must have complete and concise definition of required volumes in regard to total capacity needs and requirements. Equally important, we must also have clear and concise definition of on-time targets and order thru-put times. Lack of knowledge and understanding of the full scope of the task at hand could be disastrous!

Many times we must undertake the initiative of dissecting the total on-time service level agreement from that of the internal process for which we are accountable. For example, we must have a clear up-front agreement as to what the on-time and thru-put parameters are once all materials and specification information are available and our process segment can begin.

Often, within a total delivery process cycle, specification information is undefined, materials and components deliveries are delayed, and now instead of the normal operating three days to process the production order, it is now compressed into one! We must identify, define, and have mutual client agreement upon, again once all specification information, materials, and components are available to initiate our process segment:

- Normal process thru-put is ____ hours / days,
- Expedited process thru-put ____ hours / days,
- Maximum # or percentage of expedited orders as a component of the total production volume is ____,
- Targeted on-time production schedule delivery performance percentage is ____%.

These parameters should be clearly defined within the performance parameters of the comprehensive general operating agreement. Materials supply chains, specifications development and finalization, and resolution of non-conformance issues should typically not fall within the "bookends" of our operational accountabilities. We must have clear definition of all the above parameters so as not to overlook and/or underestimate the full scope of the total task at hand and to have all the resources needed and fully focused to achieve on-time delivery success!

d. Design and Maintenance of High-Visibility Control Board:

"In a land of blind giants, the one-eyed midget is king."

Anonymous

Visibility is an absolute essential. We must know where we are each and every hour of the production day in order to effectively manage productivity, output, and overall production schedule achievement performance. Each hour, production must be monitored, collected, recorded, posted, tracked, and variances responded to. If we can **visibly see** exactly where we are and what is going on around us, in regard to the output performance of the respective production unit, it puts us in a most improved position.

Associate work pace must be adequate, work stations and personnel added or subtracted, line speeds adjusted, equipment down-time addressed, any and all production flow constraints must be immediately identified and corrective / constructive action initiated and assertively pursued. Lost production capacity once lost in lost and cannot be regained. In addition, we in no way will consider overtime to address production capacity constraints as a viable option. Only in the case of an emergency situation and with the prior consent and approval of senior management will overtime be initiated as a solution to production capacity constraints. Remember ... the most expensive way to accomplish anything is on overtime!

Here again, process output visibility is the key management tool. Collecting and posting on a highly visible takt / display board within the respective unit (on an easel, on a wall, any area highly visible to all production associates) the hourly output volume data is essential to effective production schedule management. The design and deployment of an effective display / takt board is fairly straightforward. The basic information required should include:

- The target that is to be achieved for each hour and for the entire day / shift. These time / volume targets should be recorded and posted at the beginning of the day or shift.
- Time / hour the production data was collected and recorded.
- Actual output volume for the hour.
- Variance - hourly gain or loss verses target.
- Cumulative +/-volume performance to target as the shift / day moves forward. The cognitive dissonance created by a cumulative negative (posted in red) to target may be the only impetus required to achieve the total daily production performance goal.

- Comments on actions taken to resolve any evident constraints. This comment section also serves as a training vehicle for the entire production staff in regard to anticipation and acceptance of future corrective / constructive actions.
- This visible display also provides visibility into the in-process auditing being performed by QA personnel, leads, and/or supervisors as to:
  - Audits performed each hour,
  - # of units audited,
  - # of non-conformances detected,
  - Corrective actions initiated.

Not only does this display serve as an excellent management tool for production management, production supervision, quality assurance personnel, and all production associates; it also serves to effectively communicate to and inform the client / customer as to production unit performance each hour, of each shift, of each day. It also enhances the confidence of our client company of our skilled and responsive management of the production process. Use this highly effective process control tool and become the production management king!

d. Tracking and Communication of Production Schedule Performance:

"Talk low, talk slow, and don't say too much."

John Wayne

Via our highly visible display board that is effectively communicating our production volume performance, we can clearly see where we precisely are on hourly, shift, and daily basis. However, does anyone remember exactly how we performed yesterday, last week, last month, last quarter, or year-to-date in terms of total production schedule attainment and on-time delivery? The answer is no! And a simple run chart will serve the need most adequately.

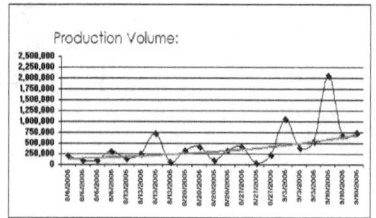

In the hustle and bustle of daily business life, many clients may not remember and/or accurately recall the consistent delivery performance achieved or the improvements that have been captured. It is up to us, in a professional and objective manner, to tell them, and to keep on telling them. While this KPI – key performance indicator - may well be included within a comprehensive performance dashboard reporting structure. However, it is nonetheless, the primary performance indicator. The product must be assembled with the highest levels of accuracy and with lowest total costs, however, if it is delivered late . . . the customer is still disappointed! We in production management and in production supervision must always remember our mission . . . "_deliver on time_, with quality excellence, at the lowest total cost."

Our consistent performance in this key measurement arena must be captured and visually communicated to _all_ stakeholders within the production output process . . . and the most important stakeholder is the client!

e. Supervisory / Lead / Production Associate Accountability:

In order to achieve the challenging task of achieving 100% of each week's respective production schedule, week after week, requires the collective, concerted efforts and initiatives of every individual within the entire work force. Everyone must do their part and totally fulfill their respective roles. Therefore, it is imperative that each individual bear production schedule volume performance attainment as a primary accountability. The basic components comprising this area of key accountability for production management, production supervision, line leads, materials coordinators, and production associates are summarized as follows:

Work Flow Management:

- Verify the production schedule for the shift, day, and week,
- Verify availability of all materials well before time to start the shift,
- Add or reduce line staffing as required,
- Constantly keep the work-in-process balanced and flowing,
- Continuously monitor the WIP (work in process) in each operation,
- Maintain production order priority and integrity,
- Must post hourly and daily production on (takt) boards by designated times,
- Monitor pace of associates. DO NOT allow pacing down for low work, etc. No idle time!

- Have a cross training plan and assure that it is followed,
- Be aware of all machine problems and how long it took to be corrected,
- Spare / balance machinery must be kept in good working order,
- Stage all completed work properly.

Everyone involved in the production process must be working concertedly together toward the achievement of required production volume output each hour of each shift of each day. It is too late to push to meet the production output demand for the shift at the last hour of the shift. It must be met or exceeded from the first hour and for each successive hour of the shift, for every shift, of every day, for the entire week.

Remember, there are three basic approaches to production management, make it happen, watch what happens, or wonder what happened! You can easily discern which one will be successful in terms of achieving customer delivery requirements and achieving sustained success.

With a through a total team approach, at each and every production level, and encompassing each functional production position, the entire production work force must be fully engaged and totally committed to delivering production schedule achievement performance excellence to the total and complete satisfaction of our client companies.

Production Flow Management

4. Production Flow Management:

a. Projection of Staffing Levels:

"There is no glory . . . in spending too much."

Anonymous

As a labor solutions provider working in within a TCM / Total Cost Management framework, we must be in control of all costs to be sure; materials, components, packaging, finished products, controllable overheads, and most importantly, labor. We must know what we need from s skills and capabilities perspective, as well as from a quantity perspective.

To review, the first component of development of overall staffing need is an understanding of the product(s) to be constructed from a complexity / familiarity perspective, from which efficiencies can be projected. The next component is to have a clear projection of production volume forecast needs that can be segmented by week, by day, by shift, and by hour. This output volume forecast demand must, from the customer's standpoint, be fully supported with the required raw materials and components that are in turn, quality assured and validated prior to line introduction. The next element is the S.A.M.'s / Standard Allowed Minute component as supplied by engineering. As we apply the appropriate math to the total production, we can, within a reasonable degree of accuracy, determine the required staffing relative to meeting the required output demand.

- ((Projected Weekly Production Volume / Available Weekly Production Hours) X Standard Allowed Minutes Per Unit) / 60 Minutes per Hour = Production Associates Required @ 100%. Projected associates required can then be divided by the anticipated efficiency achieved to yield the desired staffing levels.

- Example:
  Weekly Production Requirement: 500,000 Units
  Available Work Days: 4
  Required Units per Day: 125,000   (500,000 / 4)
  Available Shifts: 2

Required Units per Shift:	62,500	(125,000 / 2)
Available Shift Hours:	9.5	
Required Units per Hour:	6,579	(62,500 / 9.5)
S.A.M.'s Per Unit:	.800	
Required Total S.A.M.'s Per Hour:	5,263	(6,579 X .800)
Required @ 100% Efficiency:	88	(5,263 / 60)
Required @ 80% Efficiency:	110	(88 / .80)
Required @ 120% Efficiency:	61	(88 / 1.2)

A total production staff of 88 direct (an individual within the production process touches and adds real value to the finished product) associates per shift is required to assure complete and on-time delivery of the required 500,000 units for the respective production week in the above example. Note the format below:

Design of forms and data analysis should be customized for the specific application.

Staffing Needs Calculation Form:

Shift / Line Production Volume Target:
From Client's Projected Production Schedule Requirements:

Today's Date:

Available Production Hours:
Available Production Hours = Total Shift Hours - Meal Time: (Example 10 Shift Hours - 30 Minute Meal Time = 9.5 Available Hours)

Hourly Production Volume Target:
Shift Production Volume Target / Available Production Hours:

S.A.M.'s Per Unit:
Standard Allowed Minutes From IE Standards Information:

Total Work Minutes Required Per Hour @ 100%:
S.A.M.'s X Hourly Production Volume Target:

Staffing Requirements @ 100%:
Total Work Minutes Required / 60:

Projected Efficiency:
Estimated Based Upon Management Discretion and Product / Process Familiarity:

Adjusted Staffing Requirements:
Staffing Requirements @ 100% / Adjusted Efficiency %:

Management / Supervisory Signature:

52

In addition, production management must then assess, evaluate, and plan for the availability of required work stations and needed equipment. From an indirect (an individual within the production process that adds no real value to the finished product) support standpoint, management must also assess, evaluate, and plan for supervisory needs, training needs, materials coordination needs, in-process and end item auditing needs, and administrative / payroll needs as well.

Some examples of typical indirect staffing levels are expressed in terms of indirect to direct rations such as:

- Supervision: 1 supervisor per 20 direct associates,
- Leads: 1 lead per 5 to 10 production associates,
- In-Process / End-Item Auditors: 1 per 20 to 50
- Materials Coordinators: 1 per 10 to 20 production associates,
- Administrative / Payroll: 1 per 50 to 100 production associates.

The above is simply intended to serve as a general guideline. Actual production conditions, products, process variability, quality requirements, combination of fractional positions, and other factors will play a role in the final management determination of the overall indirect staffing levels and total indirect labor costs.

In the above example, it is again quite evident, the positive financial impact, from an indirect support cost perspective, of the benefit of increased efficiencies.

Also, engineering, in conjunction with production management, will provide the necessary production staffing calculations guidelines and tools for effective and ongoing labor cost management. This is the single most important controllable operational cost and it is our responsibility to manage it effectively.

b. Confirmation of Raw Materials Supplies:

"Measure twice . . . cut once."

Carpenter's Rule

It goes without saying that making a good product from inferior raw materials and components is just not possible in the vast majority of situations. It would be even more challenging to produce finished production without the required raw materials and components even being available!

It is typically within the client company's accountability and responsibility to provide raw materials and components in adequate quantity and in compliance with stated quality parameters. However, that sometimes just doesn't always happen. Nor do we in production management wish to get a line up, fully operational, and highly efficient, only to have it constrained and possibly shut-down when we find out too late, that a material and/or component failed to meet quality and/or quantity needs and parameters. How to we avoid this needless waste of time, effort, and money?

Prior to entry into the production process, all raw materials and components should be delivered into a queuing area. All respective materials and components should have adequate production order and product BOM identification. A designated individual, this could be a lead, materials coordinator, or in-process auditor must assure:

- Materials and components are appropriately identified and segregated by production order designation.
- The respective materials and components correspond with the specific production order, finished product, and BOM as designated by numerical identifiers (as many materials and components visually appear the same).
- The respective materials and components correspond with the specific production order, finished product, and BOM as designated by quantities and finished products required.
- At a minimum, (1) one case per material RM# and (1) case per component identification # are opened to confirm bulk and/or pallet items actually packed, correspond with the specific BOM.
- In-process documentation is compiled that provides adequate process traceability.

- Only with the appropriate authorizing QA / lead / materials coordination approval may the materials and components be moved into line for support of the production process.
- *All material and component non-conformances and irregularities must be addressed and resolved prior to line introduction.*
- All materials and components must be re-validated and re-confirmed by the respective production unit materials coordinator prior to positioning into the production process.

Design of forms and data analysis should be customized for the specific application.

Materials and Components Validation Form:

Production Order #:	Today's Date:	Material / Component # Matches BOM / Specification:
Order Quantity:		Materials / Components Quantities Match Production Order Quantity:
Product #:	BOM / Spec. Date:	Actual Materials / Components Packed Match Case - Carton ID:

#	Materials / Component #		Yes:	No:	If "No" - Corrective Action Implemented:
1		Verification:			
2		Verification:			
3		Verification:			
4		Verification:			
5		Verification:			
6		Verification:			
7		Verification:			
8		Verification:			
9		Verification:			
10		Verification:			

Auditor's Signature:

Supervisor's Signature:

Comments:

Use Additional Sheets If Required:

The worst case scenario is that non-conforming or inadequate materials and components are supplied into line, the line is stopped . . .

- Associates must be either re-assigned to other duties (lost productivity, lost revenue, and/or added cost),

- Associates are sent home (lost productivity, lost revenue, earnings loss for the associates, and negative morale impact),
- Non-conforming production is scattered throughout the production process (more lost productivity, lost revenue, and/or added cost),
- Inspection, re-handling, and segregation of non-conforming product and material may be required (more lost productivity, lost revenue, and/or added cost),
- Rework of the product may be required (more lost productivity, lost revenue, and/or added cost),
- Re-start of the production process is required (more lost productivity, lost revenue, and/or added cost),
- Overtime is often required to "catch up" lost production capacity (more lost productivity, lost revenue, and/or added cost).

The above are certainly not the keys to successful production management! It is indeed vital that a process of thorough validation of all incoming raw materials and components be accurately completed, documented, and appropriate corrective actions initiated prior to production process introduction. This is a cornerstone of effective production management.

c. Confirmation of Equipment Availability:

"The greatest production manager in the entire world cannot meet their production demands . . . without adequate operational equipment."

Anonymous

As we have reviewed previously, it is a critical to production schedule completion success to project total staffing needs based upon the forecasted schedule combined with engineered standards and projected efficiencies. This is also inclusive of equipment needs as well. Packing, sealing, stamping, taping, filling, printing, labeling, attaching,  testing, soldering, or any other operation that requires that one or more mechanical devices be employed at any given point within the production process, that equipment must be deployed in adequate numbers in order to facilitate the required hourly production flow rate.

In our previous example, the hourly flow rate was projected to be 6,579 units. Assuming a S.A.M. (Standard Allowed Minute) value of .125 for the specific machine operation, which would in turn equate to:

6,579 unit flow per hour X .125 S.A.M. = 822 work minutes / 60 minutes per hour = 13.7 machines required at 100% efficiency. Here again actual numbers may require adjustment based upon projected efficiencies being higher or lower. And, since we cannot deploy .7 machines this would equate to 14 total machines required at 100% at this production level. Also to be considered is that machines malfunction, parts break, servicing and maintenance is required, and therefore it is highly recommended that an additional "provisional" machine be added for these normal occurrence factors, thereby bringing the total machine / equipment in this scenario to 15.

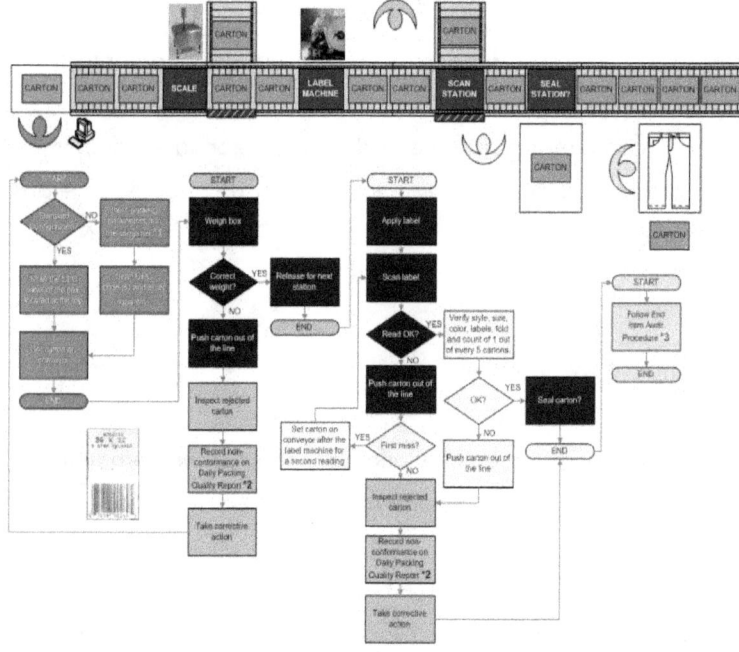

An absolutely critical success factor is the appropriate hourly production flow rate must be consistent across and through all operations, manual and well as machine / equipment specific.

An exception may be made wherein the costs of equipment may be capital intensive and therefore cost prohibitive. In that situation a work-in-process buffer and queuing area may be created to facilitate manual operations being performed on a single shift which in turn supply equipment / machine specific operations that are performed on 2 or more corresponding shifts. However, this may require additional handling and transportation costs, as well as floor space, as the product must be off-loaded into some type of internal storage vehicle or platform, moved into a staging / queuing area, and possibly moved again out of the staging area into the machine / equipment specific operational area.

Therefore, before a solid commitment can be made relative to the full attainment of a desired level of production with corresponding daily and weekly production schedule and delivery volumes; calculation, validation, and full confirmation of available operational equipment must be accurately and thoroughly completed. This confirmation must fully involve and be fully agree to by both the responsible on-site production manager and the operational management of the client company. This above recommended approach best assures full and complete client satisfaction and total operational success from a production schedule completion and on-time delivery standpoint as it is impacted upon by required machinery and equipment demands.

d. Operational Work Flow Balance (Theory of Constraints):

"Just as a chain is no stronger than its weakest link . . . a production process is no faster than its slowest single operation."

Anonymous

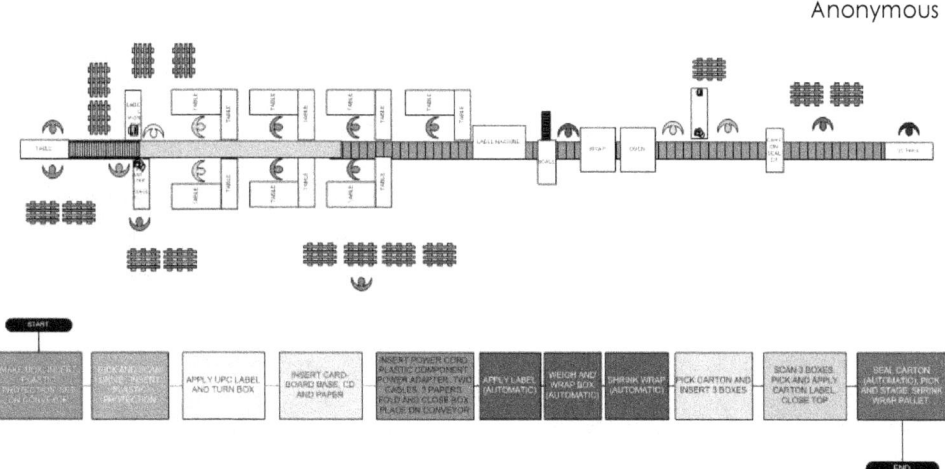

For the above illustrated assembly and packaging process to perform at optimum effectiveness and efficiency, one critical element must be recognized and structured into the design of the total line structure and staffing level. Each operational segment within the process must maintain a consistent rate of unit completion volume flow. Otherwise, the entire process is sub-optimized as the end output can only equal the unit volume that is processed through the slowest, least efficient single operation. In the above illustration, the 16 total production associates can only produce at a rate that is consistent with the least productive operation and/or associate. That can be extremely costly. And that is what the theory of constraints is all about!

Of course, no production process has infinite volume capability. At some given volume level, the theory of constraints will impact upon one or more of the operational segments within the process. As that constraint is identified and lifted or removed, production volumes can then be increased. However volumes can only be increased up to the volume level of the next constraining operation in regard to the available capacity of that specific process segment.

This cycle of identification and lifting of a specific constraint, only to identify and lift the next constrain, and so on, until you are back at your original, initial constraining operation, is an integral component of the continuous improvement process as it related to production capacities.

e. **Effective Planning and Execution of Shift Start-Up:**

"One does not plan to fail . . . they usually fail to plan."

Anonymous

Just as in a race, it is critical to get off to a solid start and playing catch-up can be difficult if not impossible. It is the very same situation with the start-up of a production shift. Everything must begin moving forward immediately at the starting bell! Materials, equipment, and production personnel must all be in place . . . ready . . . and set . . . to go . . . at the very beginning of each shift. Catch-up is not possible. Lost production volume and capacity cannot be somehow recaptured when lost. Lost production capacity and corresponding volume also result in lost revenue and lost earnings potential for the production associates that cannot be regained.

Therefore, it is imperative that as production management has a number of areas; materials, equipment, specifications, and production associates that must be effectively coordinated, a planned, systematic approach is an indispensable element to success. That planned systematic approach includes:

- Each shift supervisor and/or shift lead should view the next shift as close partners and the combined performance of all shifts is necessary for the total success of our client company – as we as that of our own organization.

- The previous shift supervisor and/or shift lead should have all specifications, samples, production status information, equipment conditions, and any other mission critical information prepared for the supervision of the subsequent shift.

- The previous shift supervisor and/or shift lead should have any component deficiency information, product quality information, machine trouble, or any other performance critical information prepared for the supervision of the subsequent shift.

- The shift supervisor, and/or shift lead, and materials coordinators should be in the department 30 to 60 minutes prior to the shift start up to assure and confirm production orders scheduled for upcoming shift, review / confirm materials availability, review / confirm equipment up/down status, review and confirm line staffing plans, and review / confirm overall staffing needs.

- The shift supervisor and/or shift lead should initiate any needed corrective actions to address any short-falls or deficiencies in any of the above areas so that all scheduled production orders may be completed. The supervisor should immediately seek management assistance if their efforts fail to achieve desired results in regard to resolution of any above issues. If issues persist that will impact upon production order completion performance, then staffing levels should be adjusted immediately.

- The shift supervisor and/or shift lead should establish hourly production targets by line for each product.

- The shift supervisor and/or shift lead should monitor hourly production achieved verses targets by line for each product. Corrective actions should be immediately pursued as any shortfalls are noted.

- All required production documentation and shift hand-off information should be completed fully, accurately, and on time by the appropriate shift supervisor and/or shift lead.

A typical shift hand-off format may appear as follows:

Design of forms and data analysis should be customized for the specific application.

Shift Start-Up & Hand-Off Check Sheet:

Date:		Shift:			Shift Supervisor:	
Shift Production Order Schedule Confirmed:			Yes:	No:	Issues:	
Order Numbers Produced:						
Order Numbers Produced:						
Accurate Samples / Specifications Available:			Yes:	No:	Corrective Actions:	
Components / Materials Confirmed:			Yes:	No:	Corrective Actions:	
Noted Deficiencies / Short-Falls:						
Machine Availability Confirmed:			Yes:	No:	Corrective Actions:	
Noted Deficiencies / Short-Falls:						
Line Staffing Confirmed:			Yes:	No:	Corrective Actions:	
Noted Deficiencies / Short-Falls:						
Product Quality Issues:			Yes:	No:	Corrective Actions:	
Noted Deficiencies / Short-Falls:						
Other Key Issues / Concerns:						
					Hand-Off Made to:	

It is vital that mission critical information be effectively up-front communicated so that the subsequent shift start-up is in no way delayed due to communication failures or other situations that would create time-loss / capacity loss situations for the subsequent shift supervisor and other shift production personnel.

There may be occasions wherein the urgency of inherent production related issues may push one into thinking that I am just too busy to do this. You must not allow the urgent to push aside the important. Capturing all available production capability and translating that into on-time delivery for our client company, into increased earnings potential for our associates, and into increased revenues for JCS Logistics is of the very highest priority and importance!

f. Planning and Execution of Next-Order Set-Up:

"Everything comes to him who hustles while he waits."

Thomas Edison

Just as with an effective shift start-up, effective production order / line product changeover is an essential element in regard to capturing and securing the greatest possible opportunity relative to production volume output, maximization of production associate earnings potentials, and maximization of total revenue generation potential for JCS Logistics.

Well in advance of the end of the current production run for a specific production order or product, the effective supervisor, in close partnership and collaboration with the respective materials coordinator must:

- Identify the next available production order within the production order priority sequence,

- Acquire the appropriate production order / product specification information for the next order in the production priority sequence,

- Initiate acquisition and validation of materials and components,

- Confirm line location, configuration, and staffing requirements,

- Complete materials and components validation and complete pre-location into appropriate and sequential production assembly positions,

- As previous line sequentially completes the previous production order, reposition / realign front end operational personnel into new line configuration in construction assembly sequence,

- Continue sequential relocation / realignment of production personnel until all production staff is positioned into the new production line configuration,

- Perform QA verification of first-off and continue heavy sampling on initial production until line stability is achieved and assured.

The responsible supervisor and the responsible materials coordinator must "hustle" to assure effective pre-production validation and set-up of the next production order the appropriate production priority sequence. "Waiting" on the part of any of the production associates must absolutely be minimized. This, in turn, allows additional production capability, improved on-time delivery, increased associates earnings potential, and increased revenues to come to JCS Logistics!

g. Performance Manager / Supervisor / Lead / Materials Coordinator Accountability:

"For truly, if the trumpet sounds an indistinct call, who will get ready for battle?"

Apostle Paul

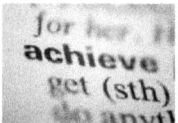
As managers, engineers, supervisors, leads, materials coordinators, and administrators, we are all here to achieve a common goal, to pursue a common mission. Our purpose must be clear and concise. Our applied energies must be concerted and focused. Therefore, the following accountabilities are structured to be mutually supportive and directed toward a single common purpose of providing excellence in products and services to our client companies, fair opportunities for all associates, and a reasonable profit for our organization.

Our Mission:

As managers, supervisors, leads, and engineers, our first and primary responsibility is to our client companies and to the purchasers and users of the products and services we provide. In meeting their needs, everything we do must be of the highest quality. We must constantly strive to reduce our costs in order to maintain reasonable and competitive pricing.

Secondly, we are responsible to our associates, the men and women working with us at every level of our organization. We must respect their dignity and recognize their merit. Compensation must be fair and adequate. Working conditions must be clean, orderly, and safe. Associates must feel free to make suggestions and surface opportunities for improvement. There must be equal opportunity for employment, development, and advancement for those qualified. We must provide competent management and our actions must be just and ethical.

Thirdly, we are responsible to the communities in which we live and work. We must be good citizens supporting good works and encouraging improvement. We must maintain in good order the property we are privileged to use and protect the environment we work within.

Fourthly, our final responsibility is to our company. Our business must be fiscally sound. We must experiment with new ideas. Innovation must be embraced, progressive programs developed, new methods deployed, and new services introduced.

When we operate according to these principles, we will promote continued success.

Performance Manager - Accountabilities:

The performance management position is responsible for providing leadership, direction and control of the production department(s) or unit(s). It is accountable for the attainment of all revenue, cost, output, and efficiency goals and objectives as set forth in the general operating plan pertaining to product manufacture, finished product quality, and control and reduction of total costs. In addition to functional responsibilities, it shares accountability for the overall direction of the production unit or department with the industrial engineer. This is accomplished through the execution of the following accountabilities:

- **Customer Service:**
    - Assure attainment of daily / weekly production schedules.
    - Work with client's other departments to develop cross-functional relationships.
    - Support general operating plan revenue generation initiatives.
    - Assure control of WIP, cycle times, quick response, and inventory levels.
    - Assure weekly progress review meetings are conducted with the client company's management.

- **Product Quality:**
    - Assure effective systems to provide finished product and process quality that meets or exceeds client's requirements.
    - Perform random in-process sampling as required for general application, specific products, specific operations, and specific associates.
    - Collect, analyze, and track key QA data at the associate and operational levels to assure focused and effective corrective action.

- **Cost Control and Reduction:**
    - Facilitate continuous improvement in all areas of total cost.
    - Assure labor utilization efficiency of 100% or higher.
    - Assure continuous improvement in off standard labor costs.
    - Assure operating budget spending control performance.
    - Support the introduction of new technology, methods, and systems.

- Assure protection of proprietary technologies, systems, and methods.
- Assure maximization of materials utilization.
- Assure utilization, maintenance, and protection of all assets.
- Assure accurate and prompt reporting and tracking of all daily / weekly critical success factor information.

- **Safety:**
  - Assure consistent implementation of all OSHA / EPA / FDA / CLIENT COMPANY safety, ergonomic, and risk management regulations, policies, guidelines, and initiatives as they specifically relate to safe and effective operations.

- **Workforce Development:**
  - Assure effective administration all Staffmark policies, procedures, and reporting protocols.
  - Assure management and development of associate skills and capabilities.
  - Assure maintenance of high associate morale.
  - Assure maintenance of good corporate citizenship and positive customer relations.

Weekly Management Activity Plan:

Initiative	Accountability	Review
#1 Assure planning and component delivery coordination to support attainment of production schedules and revenue generation budget. Assure daily / weekly critical success factor tracking to support output performance by production unit. Accomplished through planning partnership and communication.	Manager	Weekly
#2 Assure employment levels are sustained in order	Manager	Weekly

to achieve schedule and revenue parameters thru a program of assertive recruiting, hiring, and training.			
#3 Assure deployment and set up of all workstations & equipment needed for full production schedule & revenue projection attainment by product unit. Also for new product start up.	Manager Engineer		Weekly
#4 Assure methods, standard conditions, and rate structures by operation support full production schedule attainment, to include an intensive focus on associates performing below standard.	Manager Engineer		Weekly
#5 Assure line loading by construction unit by hour to support output schedule attainment by unit & address line limitations in personnel and workstation parameters by product unit.	Manager Engineer		Weekly
#6 Continue performance-focused supervisory development programs with an intensive focus on 1st quality product generation and effective workflow management.	Manager Engineer		Weekly
#7 Assure an on-floor supervisory activity auditing / support program to assure effective focusing upon key work flow and quality management results.	Manager		Weekly
#8 Assure effective and continuing implementation	Manager		Weekly

of focused in-process sampling procedures data collection & corrective action.		
#9 Continue manager / engineer / supervisory end item auditing to confirm and assure correlation with daily in-process sampling results.	Manager Engineer Supervisors	Weekly
#10 Assure accurate and consistent supervisory in-process sampling accountability and enforcement.	Manager	Weekly
#11 Deploy training & development programs to focus on rapid performance attainment & assure all associates have an hourly / daily / weekly documented output goal plan.	Manager Engineer Supervisor	Weekly
#12 Assure that all trained and experienced associates below standard are on an hourly / daily / weekly documented goal improvement plan.	Manager Supervisors	Weekly
#13 Assure that all associates above the operational UCL have an individualized documented goal improvement plan.	Manager Engineer Supervisor	Weekly
#14 Conduct weekly off-standard reviews to analyze and evaluate options for control & reduction of no work, transfer, downtime, rework, & scrap categories.	Manager Engineer Supervisor	Weekly
#15 Assure work flow output of finished product data	Manager Engineer	Weekly

collection and posting at mid-day and end-of-day for communication and corrective action planning.	Supervisor	
#16 Analyze performance by associate & operation to facilitate solutions development and implementation.	Manager Engineer	Weekly
#17 Implementation of key performance / critical success factor goal establishment, measurement, tracking, communication and senior management review.	Manager Engineer	Weekly
#18 Establish and maintain key performance targets for all supervisors relative to schedule attainment, associates below standard, associates above UCL's, off standard control, unit efficiency, revenue generation, etc.	Manager	Weekly
#19 Support supervisory daily routine planning and Key accountabilities to include management auditing format and enforcement.	Manager	Weekly
#20 Assure documented associate performance	Manager	Weekly
improvement plans for associates below standard,		
above UCL, or with attendance issues.		

Performance Supervisor Accountabilities:

Be in the department 30 to 60 minutes before the starting time of the shift. This allows time for preparation of paper work, checking plans for balance and speaking to the associates and the customer's on-site management. Make sure plans for substitute associates are being carried out when an absence is known ahead of time. This allows for a smoother, calmer start of the day. Each associate should be in his or her assigned work place, ready to begin work at the start of the shift. Any unexpected absence must have a substitute assigned as soon as possible or other arrangements must be made. Throughout the day, monitor production for each associate within the department. This is done to determine if your department is meeting its production goals each hour and for the day. Each day the following duties should be performed (some more often than others, but all at least once).

- **Interpersonal Skills:**
    - Set a positive example for everyone in you department.
    - Greet each associate with an enthusiastic "Good Morning!"
    - Communicate constructively with associates throughout the day.
    - Praise progress and success. Express appreciation for a job well done.

- **Work Flow Management:**
    - Verify the production schedule for the day and for the week.
    - Verify availability of all materials well before time to start the line.
    - Add or reduce line staffing as required.
    - Constantly keep the work balanced and flowing.
    - Continuously monitor the WIP (work in process) in each operation.
    - Maintain production order integrity and priority.
    - Must post hourly and/or daily production on boards by designated time.
    - Monitor pace of associates. DO NOT allow pacing down for low work, etc. No idle time!
    - Have a cross training plan and see that associates are following it.
    - Be aware of all machine problems and how long it took to be corrected. Spare machinery, if available, must be kept in good working order. They may be used for repairs or cross training.

- Stage all completed work properly.

- **Quality:**
    - Monitor the quality / accuracy of work being produced. Use the in-process sampling plan developed for the specific project and/or products specified.
    - Monitor rework / repair closely. Rework / repair MUST be completed and corrected immediately.
    - All scrap must be accounted for using the appropriate form(s) provided by the customer and/or engineering.
    - Focus sampling upon operations, associates, and products with the highest percent non-conformances.

- **Workforce Development:**
    - Set hourly and daily production goals for all associates.
    - Check the method being used by each associate. Associates should use methods approved by engineering; if not, correct and ask for help from the engineer or trainer assigned to that specific project.
    - Follow-up with low performing associates. What can be done to help them improve?
    - Perform potential studies on low performing associates.
    - Determine weakest link (constraint) in the production line and offer possible solutions.
    - Monitor department analysis, efficiency, performance, and all costs areas.

- **Safety & Housekeeping:**
    - Keep aisles clear and safe.
    - Insure exits are NEVER blocked.
    - All machine shields and guarding must be kept in place at all times.
    - Lockout /tag-out procedures must be followed at all times.
    - All designated personal protective equipment (PPE) must be worn at all times.
    - Electrical safety protocols must be followed at all times.

- Insure the general cleanliness of each workstation and the entire department.

- **Problem Solving:**
    - Be proactive, NOT reactive.
    - Be alert to all off standard situations and why they occurred.
    - Completely handle one problem before moving on to another.
    - REMEMBER!! HOW ARE WE DOING NOW? HOW CAN WE IMPROVE?

- **Communication:**
    - Advise manager of potential problems before they happen. Ex. Not meeting schedule, quality, etc.
    - Turn in all payroll and production reports promptly, on time, and accurately.
    - ASK FOR HELP WHEN NEEDED!

Lead Accountabilities:

Be in the department 30 to 60 minutes before the starting time of the shift. This allows time for preparation of paper work, checking plans for balance and speaking to the associates and the customer's on-site management. Make sure plans for substitute associates are being carried out when an absence is known ahead of time. This allows for a smoother, calmer start of the day. Each associate should be in his or her assigned work place, ready to begin work at the start of the shift. Any unexpected absence must have a substitute assigned as soon as possible or other arrangements must be made. Throughout the day, monitor production for each associate within the department. This is done to determine if your department is meeting its production goals each hour and for the day. Each day the following duties should be performed (some more often than others, but all at least once).

- **Interpersonal Skills:**
    - Set a positive example for everyone in you department.
    - Greet each associate with an enthusiastic "Good Morning!"
    - Communicate constructively with associates throughout the day.
    - Praise progress and success. Express appreciation for a job well done.

- **Work Flow Management:**
    - Verify the production schedule for the day and for the week.
    - Verify availability of all materials well before time to start the line.
    - Add or reduce line staffing as required.
    - Constantly keep the work balanced and flowing.
    - Continuously monitor the WIP (work in process) in each operation.
    - Maintain production order integrity and priority.
    - Must post hourly and/or daily production on boards by designated time.
    - Monitor pace of associates. DO NOT allow pacing down for low work, etc. No idle time!
    - Have a cross training plan and see that associates are following it.
    - Be aware of all machine problems and how long it took to be corrected. Spare machinery, if available, must be kept in good working order. They may be used for repairs or cross training.

- Stage all completed work properly.

- **Quality:**
    - Monitor the quality / accuracy of work being produced. Use the in-process sampling plan developed for the specific project and/or products specified.
    - Monitor rework / repair closely. Rework / repair MUST be completed and corrected immediately.
    - All scrap must be accounted for using the appropriate form(s) provided by the customer and/or engineering.
    - Focus sampling upon operations, associates, and products with the highest percent non-conformances.

- **Workforce Development:**
    - Set hourly and daily production goals for all associates.
    - Check the method being used by each associate. Associates should use methods approved by engineering; if not, correct and ask for help from the engineer or trainer assigned to that specific project.
    - Follow-up with low performing associates. What can be done to help them improve?
    - Perform potential studies on low performing associates.
    - Determine weakest link (constraint) in the production line and offer possible solutions.
    - Monitor department analysis, efficiency, performance, and all costs areas.

- **Safety & Housekeeping:**
    - Keep aisles clear and safe.
    - Insure exits are NEVER blocked.
    - All machine shields and guarding must be kept in place at all times.
    - Lockout /tag-out procedures must be followed at all times.
    - All designated personal protective equipment (PPE) must be worn at all times.
    - Electrical safety protocols must be followed at all times.

- Insure the general cleanliness of each workstation and the entire department.

- **Problem Solving:**
    - Be proactive, NOT reactive.
    - Be alert to all off standard situations and why they occurred.
    - Completely handle one problem before moving on to another.
    - REMEMBER!! HOW ARE WE DOING NOW? HOW CAN WE IMPROVE?

- **Communication:**
    - Advise manager of potential problems before they happen. Ex. Not meeting schedule, quality, etc.
    - Turn in all payroll and production reports promptly, on time, and accurately.
    - ASK FOR HELP WHEN NEEDED!

Materials Coordinator Accountabilities:

Be in the department 30 to 60 minutes before the starting time of the shift. This allows time for preparation and checking plans for balance and speaking to the associates. Each day the following duties should be performed (some more often than others, but all at least once).

- **Interpersonal Skills:**
    - Set a positive example for everyone in you department.
    - Greet each associate with an enthusiastic "Good Morning!"
    - Communicate constructively with associates throughout the day.

- **Work Flow Management:**
    - Verify the production schedule for the day and for the week.
    - Verify availability of all materials well before time to start the line.
    - Constantly keep the work balanced and flowing.
    - Continuously monitor the WIP (work in process) in each operation.
    - Maintain production order integrity.
    - Be aware of all machine problems.
    - Stage all completed work properly.

- **Quality:**
    - Monitor the quality of work being produced. Use the in-process sampling plan developed for the specific project and/or products specified.
    - Monitor rework / repair closely. Rework / repair MUST be completed and corrected immediately.
    - All scrap must be accounted for using the appropriate form(s) provided by the customer and/or engineering.
    - Focus QA sampling upon operations, associates, and products with the highest percent non-conformances.

- **Safety & Housekeeping:**
    - Keep aisles clear and safe.
    - Insure exits are NEVER blocked.
    - All machine shields and guarding must be kept in place and in use at all times.
    - Lockout /tag-out procedures must be followed at all times.
    - All designated personal protective equipment (PPE) must be worn at all times.
    - Electrical safety protocols must be followed at all times.
    - Support the general cleanliness of the department.

- **Problem Solving:**
    - Be proactive, NOT reactive.
    - Be alert to all off standard situations and why they occurred.
    - Completely handle one problem before moving on to another.
    - REMEMBER!! HOW ARE WE DOING NOW? HOW CAN WE IMPROVE?

- **Communication:**
    - Advise manager of potential problems before they happen. Ex. Not meeting schedule, quality, etc.
    - ASK FOR HELP WHEN NEEDED!

Associate Performance Management

5. **Associate Performance Management:**

a. Definition of Ideal Associate Profile:

"Rule # 249 . . . Hire people smarter than you."

Life's Little Instruction Book

This is undoubtedly one of the most vital managerial and leadership functions that you will perform. Your future, as well as that of your organization, is directly related to the effectiveness of your management of the hiring process. In his book *Success Is a Choice*, Rick Pitino states that his personal number one priority and the activity that he personally devotes more time to than any other, is the recruiting of talented players for his team. And as the winningest coach in college basketball and as the highest paid coach in professional basketball, he must know what he is talking about!

Just as an effective hiring process can support the creation and maintenance of winning teams, conversely, poor management of your hiring process, hiring mistakes, can be very costly and at times very painful. In order to establish and maintain a successful, vigorous, and effective hiring process, it is absolutely vital that functional management establish and maintain a strong and collaborative partnership with the human resource function.

It is of vital importance that the specific needs of the work environment be identified, quantified to the extent possible, and the corresponding worker characteristics, skills, and behaviors critical to success correspondingly be identified as well. Within the typical manufacturing and distributions environments, the following required attributes / ideal associate profile are typical:

- High levels of attendance and punctuality – 95% or greater,
- Proficient arm-hand-eye-leg-foot coordination and dexterity,
- Physical proficiency to maintain a production work pace for 8+ hours,
- Flexibility to be available to work reasonable overtime,
- Capability to lift up to 35 pounds,
- Comfortable in fast-paced, team environment,
- Proficient alpha-numeric recognition capability,
- Fundamental grasp of inter-personal skills (manners),

- Positive, can-do attitude.

Hiring and positioning the best possible skill and talent that is available is a highly critical component to overall operational success. We must clearly identify the skills and capabilities that are required for success within the work environment. We must next diligently recruit and screen for those individuals demonstrating those required attributes. And just like an effective coach, we then must best position those individuals for maximization of their capabilities. As we capture and deploy the very best individuals available, with the appropriate talents and skills, we will insure that we will have a winning team!

b. Appropriate Screening and Selection of Production Associates:

"The single best indicator of future performance . . . is past achievement."

"On Hiring" by Robert Half

In my own personal experience, I can underscore and reinforce the truthfulness of Mr. Half's statement above. As an individual can provide adequate evidence of past achievement, there is an overwhelming probability that individual will continue a similar pattern of achievement on into the future.

Once all information has been collected, a final hiring decision that is in both the best interests of the individual under consideration and your organization must be reached. Considering your exposure to this prospective candidate, do they, to a reasonable degree, demonstrate these positive characteristics?

- Punctual,

- Makes reasonable eye contact,

- Enthusiastic, energetic,

- Demonstrates interest,

- Work history demonstrates reliability, dependability, and progressive professional and/or financial advancement,

- Appears to possess mental and physical capabilities to perform the essential functions of the job,

- Demonstrates good listening skills,

- Demonstrates ability to follow instructions,

- Well mannered.

Assure that input from all the individuals within your organization exposed to this prospective associate, the receptionist, individual verifying references, all individuals involved in interviewing process, are included in a collaborative effort to achieve the best hiring decision possible. Are you now reasonably convinced that this individual has a good opportunity to succeed in the job for which they are being considered? If not, continue looking. Please don't set up a set of conditions wherein that individual, the organization, and possibly you are likely to fail. Set your people, your production associates, and yourself up to win!

c. Methods Training and Work Pace Hardening:

"Production is not the application of tools to material . . . but logic to work."
Peter Drucker

There is a best and logical way to approach the successful completion of a specified task or set of tasks. As production managers, supervisors, and engineers, it is our mission to constantly strive to explore, investigate, test, define, and train that "best" methodology of the work at hand. It is OUR responsibility. It is NOT the responsibility of each individual production associate, on their own, to somehow determine what that "best" and most logical methodology is for themselves individually.

In order to optimize the productive capability of the work force, the facilities, and the equipment that we have employed, the "best" and most logical methodology must be adequately developed. This does require the efforts, inputs, and initiative of the client company, management, supervision, quality assurance, engineering, as well as the associates themselves. To be inclusive within the methodology for a specific task the following areas must be encompassed:

- Associate safety,
- Product quality,
- Materials utilization,
- Time / motion economy,
- Ergonomic, balanced motion,
- Equipment / machinery interface,
- Work and floor space utilization,
- WIP / Work-In-Process Levels,
- Thru-Put / cycle time,
- Equipment / machine utilization.

Relative to a specific and/or specialized application, there may be additional considerations.

Therefore, it is well evident that defining and training the "best" and most logical methodology is a collective, total manufacturing team effort in order to achieve the optimum economic balance in consideration of all of the above factors. And therefore, full compliance and cooperation from each production team associate member is not optional. We must all work collectively, in concert, as a total production team to effectively deliver required products and services, on time, with quality excellence, and at the lowest total cost.

In regard to work pace hardening, this is very similar to the development that a runner or perhaps any endurance athlete must go through to be a winner. With the manufacturing and distribution work environments, muscles are used and ranges of motions are performed that impact significantly the body's muscle-skeletal structure. It is a matter of developing endurance, production pace endurance.

d. Individual / Team / Line Hourly Production Goals:

"Your people will generally live up . . . or live down . . . to your expectations."

Anonymous

There is a very basic human psychological mechanism at work relative to the establishment and attainment of realistic goals. It is termed, "cognitive dissonance." That is that little feeling inside that makes us feel somewhat uncomfortable when we see that we and/or our team has fallen below our goal, that our customer is disappointed, and that our financial rewards are diminished.

However, when we attain or exceed our goals, we know that we have pleased our customer, our financial rewards have improved, and we have that feeling of deep satisfaction . . . that is the opposite side of cognitive dissonance and it make us feel very good. We, as effective managers, supervisors, and engineers must put the psychological mechanism for our mutual and collective benefit.

Mr. Zig Ziglar put is like this, what I you put a blindfold on an expert marksman and the required them to precisely hit a specific target. As Zig puts it, "You can no more hit a target that you cannot see . . . than a target that you do not have."

We as the managers, supervisors, and leaders of the production work force, we must provide clear, concise, and achievable individual, team, line, and shift targets so that our associates will know what it takes to be successful and when they have achieved it. In doing so, we have also set up a condition wherein our associates can achieve and win! This, in turn, provides us as managers and supervisors an opportunity to provide positive feedback, reinforcement, recognition, and praise.

"There are two things people what more than money and sex . . . . it is recognition and praise."

Mary Kay Ashe

Who can deny the success of Mary Kay! Let set our associates up to win and be recognized and praised for their collective achievement.

e. Management of Effective Associate Work Pace:

"Remember who won the race . . . the tortoise!"

We all remember the old story of the tortoise and the hare. The hare, while much faster in short bursts of speed, failed to appreciate the consistency and persistence of the tortoise. The hare wasted time, goofed off so to speak, took naps, and failed to get across the finish line ahead of that persistent and determined tortoise.

Our finish line is the end of the shift. Our key measurement is how much we have accomplished before we go home at the end of the work day. An individual associate may be fast working, however, if they start late, take extended break and meal times, take numerous personal breaks, have a high re-work percentage (remember the most inefficient way to do anything is over again), spends excessive time socializing, and stops work well before the end of the shift, what has really, in total, been accomplished?

Consistency of work pace is our focus. We desire a work pace and corresponding methodology to be ergonomically correct, safe, and sustainable for a minimum of 8 hours, allowing for appropriate and managed breaks and rest periods. The key is the establishment of a comfortable, consistent, and sustainable work rhythm. Many associates like to work to music which aids them in the establishment and maintenance of a good work rhythm.

While we expect an associate's work pace to be comfortable, safe, rhythmic, and sustainable, we do not expect it to be lethargic. A turtle is even much faster than a snail!

A good rule of thumb is that an experienced associate can be expected to perform at a pace of a touch per second - grasp a small object, move the object to a specific location, and place the object into position – per second. Try this, draw a 12" square on a table. Take and hold a deck of cards in front of you in your left hand. With your right hand, grasp and remove a single card from the deck and place it at the 1st corner of the square. Repeat the process as you place a card on each of the corners of the square repeatedly until you have used all of your cards. As you put each card down say to yourself, one Mississippi, two Mississippi, and so on. It takes approximately one (1) second to say "one Mississippi" and so forth. Now that wasn't hard at all now was it?

Of course, we will allow reasonable time for a new production associate to become pace-hardened, developing the physical stamina to maintain a consistent production pace throughout the entire shift. However, we also must be realistic, the demands of a production environment are not for everyone. After a reasonable training and orientation period, if an individual is not capable of achieving minimal production pace targets, then from a budget and cost perspective, we cannot continue to financially subsidize an associate with low efficiency. If reasonable corrective / constructive actions fail to remedy the situation, other alternatives such as job reassignment and/or possible termination of employment must be considered.

With the managed application of a rhythmic work pace consistently applied over the entire shift, with appropriate beaks and rest periods, combined with accuracy of execution, by each of our associates, we will be great aided to efficiently and cost effectively achieve our delivery and financial targets.

f. Coaching and Positive Reinforcement:

"If anything goes bad, I did it. If anything goes semi-good, then we did it. If anything goes real good, then you did it. That's all it takes to get people to win football games."

Paul "Bear" Bryant

Why should you try to catch people doing things right?
What should be an integral part of your daily management routine?
What should you generously and freely give away?
What should you strive to increase?
What is the greatest management principle in the world?

A series of studies performed by Dr. Lawrence Lindahl in the late 40's & repeated in 1991 by Ken Kovach & Bob Nelson found these issues were of the highest priority to employees.

- Full appreciation for work done,
- Feeling "in" on things,
- Sympathetic to personal problems,
- Job security,

- Good wages,
- Interesting work,
- Promotion / growth opportunity,
- Personal loyalty to workers,
- Good working conditions,
- Tactful discipline.

In a recent study conducted by Dr. Gerald Graham of Wichita State University the following was revealed as the five top workplace incentives according to the employees.

- Personnel thanks from their manager,
- Written thanks from their manager,
- Promotion for performance,
- Public praise,
- Morale building meetings.

Your responsibility as a manager and leader is to make your people feel valued. In turn they will want to give their best efforts, every day. You must make it a priority. You must proactively look for ways to recognize, praise, and reward your people.

Or as Dr. Ken Blanchard stated, "Catch people doing things right!" It is vital to your success and achievement as a managers and leaders to make a part of your regular professional routine, the practice of catching people doing thing right. Then you recognize and praise them for it.

What are some ways you can, formally and informally, recognize and praise your people at low to no cost? First, for recognition & praise to be fully effective it should encompass the following:

- It must be specific,
- The praise may be applied to individual, teams, departments, or the entire organization,
- It must be totally honest, genuine, and sincere,
- You praise and commendation must never be used to manipulate,
- It must come from you as the responsible manager.

Some other considerations as to the vehicle to deliver you commendation:

- A letter from you on formal stationary,
- A tangible reminder of a performance or key event,
- You could utilize a plague, pen, or other desk or work item,
- It should be a gift the recipient will utilize and appreciate,
- You might just ask the recipient what they may like.

Your people may not need a raise as much as they do a personal thanks for a job well done from you. Following in order of priority are the top ten motivators:

- Provide Personal Thanks: One on one, in writing or both. Do it timely, often, and sincerely.

- Make Time for Your People: Meet with and listen to your people, as much as they need or want.

- Provide Specific Feedback: About the performance of the individual, the department, and the organization. Catch your people doing things right!

- Create an Open Environment: Create a work environment wherein people feel open to express their thoughts and opinions, can be trusting, and have fun. Encourage innovation, new ideas, and individual and team initiative.

- Provide Information: How is the organization financially? What new products and services are coming? How does each individual fit into the overall plan?

- Involve Your People: Especially in those decisions that will impact them and the implementation includes them.

- Reward Performers: Advancement should be based upon performance. Support those with marginal performance in improvement or outplacement.

- Develop a Sense of Ownership: Promote, initiate, and allow your people to have a sense of involvement, participation, pride in their work, and pride in the work environment.

- Provide Opportunities to Develop New Skills: Give you people a chance to learn new skills and capabilities. Create partnerships. Help all individuals achieve goals that are compatible with and supportive of each other's goals and the organization's goals.

- Celebrate Successes: The achievements of individuals, departments, and the organization must be recognized, praised, and rewarded. Invest generously in morale and team building activities. Increase the *fun factor*!

Just a few words on rewards.

The greatest management principle in the world . . . things that get rewarded get done.
Michael Leboeuf

The basic procedure for training the killer whales that most of us have seen performing is of interest. First, the trainer begins with the bar to be jumped on the bottom of the tank. The killer whale swims over it, not too hard. The whale gets a fish. That's a good deal! The bar is slightly raised off the bottom of the tank. The whale swims over it. They get a fish. Good deal! This progressive training process is continued until the bar is at the surface of the water. The killer whale jumps over the bar, gets a fish, good deal! Once the trainer has built the necessary rapport with the killer whale, stroking the whale's tongue also becomes a part of the reward system. Be careful with that one. This progressive training continues until the bar is now several feet in the air. The killer whale jumps it, gets a fish and a stroke on the tongue, great deal, and everybody's happy including the crowd. There's not much excitement for the crowd in watching a whale swim over a bar on the bottom of the tank!

We as human work much the same way. What is it that you are rewarding? What's in it for your people to do the things you want them to do in terms of positive rewards?

Energize, motivate, and excite your people by providing positive rewards in regard to those things, your customer-centered goals, which you want to accomplish.

Reward progress, notable achievement, and goal attainment. What can those rewards be?

- Recognition and praise from you,
- Special projects,
- Preferred job assignments,
- Specialized training,
- Business related gifts,
- Promotional opportunity and advancement,
- Bonuses and pay increases.

You must recognize progress, notable achievement, and goal attainment. You must "catch our people doing things right." Make this an integral part of your daily management routine. Generously, specifically, and sincerely praise progress, notable achievement, and incremental goal attainment. Celebrate successes by investing generously in morale and team building activities. Have a party. Increase the *fun factor*! Things that get rewarded get done, so establish rewards that reinforce the attitudes, behaviors, and accomplishments you want.

This is the most powerful and effective tool for unleashing the power of the workforce upon the path to achieving the objectives that are vital to organizational success.

g. Decision Making / Corrective Action Management:

In any moment of decision the best thing you can do is the right thing. The worst thing you can do is nothing."

Theodore Roosevelt

What is a sound decision making methodology?
What are the key factors of decision making structure and direction?
What is an effective decision-team structure?
What is the decision implementation five step process?

Why is this a key human management skill?

You naturally want to decide to do the right things. What's right for your customer? What's right for your company? What's right for your people? What's right for you? This is often a complex equation to resolve. Abdication, denial, and no decision are the worst things you can do as Mr. Roosevelt stated. Yet so many factors and variables come into play:

- The number of decisions made,
- The criteria used for making the decision,
- The involvement and input of others in decisions made,
- The reactions to and effects of those decisions.

During the course of a week, how many significant decisions do you have to routinely make? What system and criteria do you use for decision making? What opportunities for input and involvement are there before your decisions are made and finalized? What are the typical reactions to and effects of your decisions? There can be and should be a structured and systematic process, a specific and effective methodology you utilize when making decisions. The key factors of decision making structure should encompass the following areas:

- **Identify the Goal or End Result You Wish to Achieve:**
    - Who is the customer?
    - What are their needs, requirements, and concerns?
    - What do we want to accomplish and ultimately achieve?
    - What is the goal?
    - Also consider and evaluate, how much time do you have in order to make the best decision practical?
    - When do you need to act?

You should be proactive and get the information you need. It is often good to slow things down. You usually have more time than you initially think that you do. Negotiate if you think more time is needed in order for you to reach a solid decision. What is to be gained by delivering a decision before it is needed? What is to be gained by investing the time to fully evaluate the issues, explore options and alternatives, solicit input from other involved or informed sources, and trial test pre-selected options? A great deal!

- **Identify Who Will Be Involved in the Implementation or Who Has a Vested Interest in the Outcome:**

    Ask yourself, from among our process, professional, or product / service customers, who should be a part of the decision making process, or included within the team member structure? Determine what specialized expertise, not already on the decision making team, you may need to include as a part of the total team. Is financial, legal, human resource, engineering, mechanical, sales, marketing, systems, etc. expertise required in order to make a sound decision?

- **With the Decision Making Team in Place, Reconfirm and Redefine the Goal or Results That Are to Be Achieved:**
    - Reconfirm, who is the customer?
    - What are their needs & concerns?
    - What must be accomplished, ultimately achieved?
    - What is the goal?

With this decision-team structure in place and utilized, poor or inappropriate decisions become harder to make. These individuals on your decision making team, as your partners and team members, also want what's in the customer's, organization's, employee's, and your collective long-term best interests. All must recognize that success is mutual and long-term. Everyone must think win-win.

"We may have come on different ships, but we are all in the same boat now."

Dr. Martin Luther King

Your decision-team structure is in place. Your customer-centered goals and results are clearly defined. The decision making five step process involves:

- **Investigate and Define the Issues:**
    - Clearly describe the problem,
    - Listen to and understand all sides,

- o Focus on data and measurement,
- o Specify items and issues, not blame,
- o Determine scope or size of the issue,
- o Quantify the goal(s), the result to be achieved,
- o Determine the measure of completion,
  - (How will you know it's corrected? This could be percentage of improvement from a baseline, a selected numerical target, an indices, etc.)
- o Target the resolution date.

- **Fix (Temporarily) the Problem:**
  - o Temporarily patch the process to keep going,
  - o Protect customers and employees,
  - o This solution is not to be totally cost effective,
  - o It is not a permanent solution.

- **Identify the Root Cause(s):**
  - o Chart or map the dysfunctional process,
  - o Review all customer needs and requirements,
  - o Look for threads of similarity / commonality,
  - o Look for opportunity for mishap,
  - o Construct a cause and effect diagram,
  - o Develop a Praeto (80% / 20% rule) analysis.

- **Take Constructive / Corrective Action:**
  - o Generate all possible solutions,
  - o Evaluate and select the most practical solution,
  - o Identify least complexity and cost,
  - o Identify least time requirement,
  - o Identify which solution provides best prevention,
  - o Determine which solution is the most implementable,
  - o Plan, document, and communicate implementation,
  - o Implement corrective action plan,
  - o Document, track, and communicate progress.

- **Evaluate and Follow Up:**

- Appraise effectiveness of your implementation relative to the predetermined measure of completion,
- Follow-up through,
  - Audits,
  - Surveys,
  - Informal communication, meetings, reviews, and feedback questions.

For an effective decision making process and structure identify the goal(s) or results you wish to achieve. Determine how much time you have in order to make the best decision practical. Identify who will be involved in the implementation and who has a vested interest in the outcome.

Determine what specialized expertise, not already on the decision making team, that you may need to include as a part of the team. With the decision-making team in place, reconfirm and / or redefine the goal(s) or results you wish to achieve.

Now you should proceed with the five step decision making process of, 1) investigate and define the issues, 2) fix (temporarily) the problem, 3) identify the root cause(s), 4) take constructive corrective action, and 5) evaluate and follow up.

Your ability to effectively make sound and implementable decisions, with the support of your people, partners, and customers, is a most critical managerial and leadership skill. It is critical to unleashing the power of the workforce upon key, customer-centered results attainment.

Work Place / Line Structure For Maximum Economy

6. Work Place / Line Structure for Maximum Economy:

a. Definition and Understanding of Product Construction:

"There is nothing so useless as doing efficiently that which should not be done at all."

Peter Drucker

How important, in working with and through our client company, that we gain a thorough and detailed understanding of the various facets of the construction of the product or the parameters of the service that we are providing.

- What is the appropriate process step sequencing?
- Is the process step sequencing critical and ridged, or flexible?
- Can process step be combined?
- May certain process steps be eliminated?
- Can the non-value-added touches, moves, and activities be reduced?

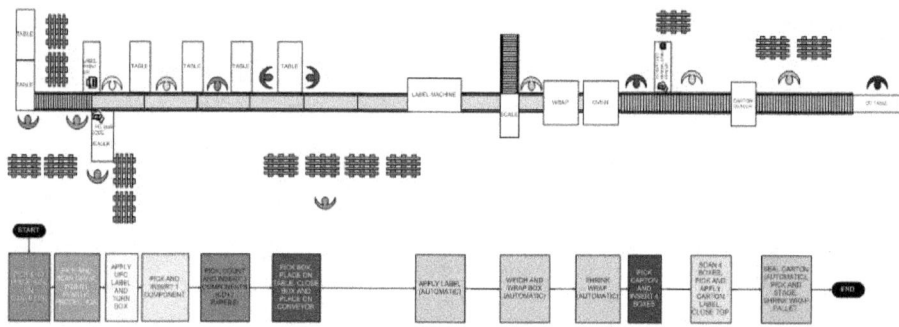

Thorough and detailed process mapping is an essential tool to processing analysis and improvement.

Having a thorough understanding of the production construction, performance parameters, and/or overall service requirement is essential. In addition, working with and through our client company within an environment of partnership and collaboration is also critical to successful evaluation, re-design, and deployment of improved processes and methods. We do well to emulate the Deming **"Plan-Do-Check-Act"** cycle which is comprised of:

- **Plan** . . . utilizing proper protocols and encompassing required approvals, structure an experimental / pilot program designed to "test" a new or innovative process improvement.

- **Do** . . . conduct the "pilot/experiment" including all appropriate measurements, checks, evaluations, observations, tests data, and information required for thorough assessment and evaluation.
- **Check** . . . complete a thorough and detailed evaluation of the experiment / pilot / test results to include all partners and stakeholders within the process and/or affected by it.
- **Act** . . . implement and deploy the process enhancement. Continue to measure, monitor, and periodically review performance to assure continuing and sustained results.

As many clients and their respective customers are demanding yearly cost-downs, this cycle of continuous re-evaluation, testing, re-design, and deployment of advancements and innovation is essential to the maintenance and health of overall process and market competitive position.

b. Work Place Arrangement for Accuracy, Efficiency, and Safety:

"Have a place for everything and keep everything in its place."

Our Mother

As children growing up, we were all strongly encouraged by our mothers to keep our rooms and closets orderly and well arranged. Have a place for everything and keep everything in its place is also excellent work place engineering advise as well.

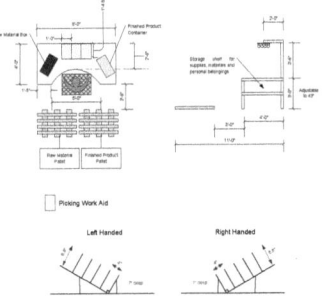

Imagine if you will, that you had to work blindfolded. Your mind, arms, and hands just had to know where things were. This is how to go about designing the ideal work place. With reasonable practice, your mind, arms, and hands unconsciously know where to reach to and grasp what to get what is needed. You do not have to look! If with each operational cycle, tools and materials were in differing positions and orientations, then the production associate would be required to stop, look around, and think-decide where what they need is, grasp it, re-orient it, and then apply it. This could potentially increase operational process cycle time as much as 100% or more!

Effective work place design checklist:

- Orderly arrangement – arranging tools and materials in order of sequential usage.
- Specific positioning of tools and materials – for blind / unconscious pick-up/retrieval, usage, and replacement to home staging position.
- Simplicity for ease of training and high levels of reliable repeatability.
- Appropriate lighting for operational execution accuracy and reduced eye / visual fatigue.
- Appropriately structured work height and reach for optimum ergonomic comfort, safely, and reduced fatigue.
- Anti-fatigue floor matting to minimize foot and leg discomfort and fatigue.
- Positioning component and materials supply and finished product staging areas in close proximity to reduce walk times and carrying distance.
- Provide appropriate ventilation and air flow to reduce heat / cold exposure, reduce fatigue, and to assure associate health and safety.
- Provide easy access to clean, cool drinking water to reduce walk distances / times, reduce fatigue and to assure associate health and safety.
- Provide appropriate hand, eye, hearing, and breathing / particulate protection as components, materials, and products require, in order to assure associate health and safety.

The work force is our single greatest operational asset. Management and engineering has the responsibility of providing a work place that is efficient, ergonomically sound, reasonably comfortable relative to the environment, and assures worker health and safety. That is the right and ethical thing to do. It is also financially the very best thing to do in regard to assuring the safety and maximum utilization of our greatest asset.

c. **OHIO:**

"... **nothing is wasted.**"

Jesus Christ / John 6:12

You might think that we are going to have a lesson in US geography or history about a state in the mid-west. Rather, OHIO stands for a most effective and powerful acronym and time / motion principle. I was on a project in a large distribution center in Plano, Texas. It was late in the evening. I was walking down a flight of stairs and there, in the stairwell, in huge letters on the wall it was written:

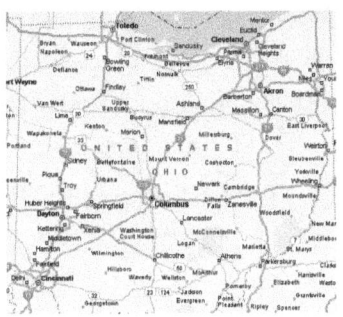

1.   O . . . nly,
2.   H . . . andle,
3.   I . . . t
4.   O . . . nce!

WOW . . . what an incredible concept that everyone can understand and help to spread throughout the production environment. Striving to structure methods and process to minimize the number of times anything is moved or handled. **The goal . . . only handle it once!**

Everyone is involved at every level and working to improve the total work environment and reduce labor costs, time, damage, and **_waste in every form_**. What an incredible concept in its simplicity and application. If you can remember OHIO – only handle it once – now everyone could be and industrial engineer and work to eliminate time, motion, and money waste!

d. Standing Verses Sitting:

"The Law of Inertia . . . things at rest tend to remain at rest; things in motion tend to remain in motion."

Over the years that I have worked within production and distribution environments, I have lost count of the times that I have seen associates sitting and waiting (waiting is totally non-value-added) for someone else to provide something for them. There was no way that they were going get up (that takes too much energy!) and get those materials or components for themselves or get up and move to help in relieving that constraining bottleneck. If the associate is sitting comfortably, they are going to tend to remain sitting at rest! In structuring our operations in this manner, we will <u>not</u> achieve our production and financial goals and targets.

Our production associates must remain on their feet and positioned so that they can readily move to fully support and facilitate continuing flows of products and material through and across each operation and process segment. Our work stations must be structured and management disciplines must support our production associates standing and moving to maximize and balance flows and efficiencies in order to have the best possible opportunity to achieve our production targets and financial goals. Our associates in motion will have the tendency to remain in motion. Stand them up and keep them and production moving!

e. Cross-Training:

"Be all that you can be."

US Army

Now that we have our skilled associates standing and moving, we must then work to create and sustain an environment wherein each individual has the opportunity to develop their skills base to the extent possible . . . be all that they can be from an operational skills standpoint.

We as managers must utilize each and every avenue to provide our associates with the opportunity to learn additional operations other than their primary job. Perhaps it may be a bit costly and sometimes uncomfortable to move a key production associate into another operation for training and development of their full skills inventory, however, this should be viewed as an investment in development of the production process.

Why make this expenditure? Turnover happens, absenteeism happens, injury happens, product configuration change happens, materials delays happen, machine downtime happens, unforeseen and unpredictable things always happen. All of this will disrupt your staffing plan if you allow it to. As successful and effective managers and supervisors, we must develop, deploy, and execute cross-training skills development plans for all associates. Then, as these factors impact upon the production process, you have the skills base and capabilities to effectively and efficiently adjust to the new production environment demands. If we do not develop, deploy, and execute cross-training and skills development plans for all associates, we will be just like the crew of the Titanic, hit the iceberg, be unprepared, and sink!

Therefore, it is a key management and supervisor accountability to create adequate opportunities for all qualified associates to develop their full range of skills and capabilities to the extent possible. In turn, that provides the production manager and production supervisor with multiple line staffing options to continue to provide on time delivery, with quality excellence, and at the lowest possible total cost, in spite of the factors that will impact upon the production environment. The answer is straightforward . . . aid and assist every production associate to "be all that they can be!"

f. Empowerment to Address the Constraint:

Now that we have structured, deployed, and are effectively executing a cross-training program, and we have our production associates being all that they can be, the next thing a skilled production manager and/or production supervisor must do is . . . . let them do it!

Unless you have the ability to be everywhere all the time, we must **empower** the production associates to move themselves up and/or down the production stream in order to address and resolve a production flow constraint. Once we have helped the production associate to well understand that when the production flow stops that their earnings opportunity is $0, they will quickly discern that it is in their best interests to do everything that we have **empowered** them to do to move to, address, and resolve the production flow constraint. That is unless you, as the production manager or supervisor, can be in all places at once all the time.

It is also vital that we as managers and supervisors must recognize and understand that production flow management is a minute-by-minute, and at times, even a second-by-second control activity. Decisions have to made every quickly and very effectively. Might I ask who is in better position to make these critical minute-by-minute decisions and take minute-by-minute actions than the qualified production associates themselves right within the production line? Who has a greater personal financial interest than they do?

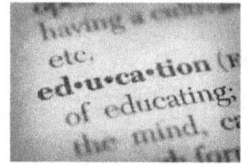
An additional critical element is that part of this developmental process includes training in communication, inter-personal, and team building skills. People don't just automatically become a team just because we tell them they are. How to courteously inter-act with team mates, common goal recognition, problem solving, and communications are vital skills that must supplement the technical / mechanical skills of the actual production process.

Positive, and may I repeat, _positive_ competition between and among the production line teams or the individual production associates themselves is also a critical element that should be facilitated by the respective production manager and/or supervisor. However, in order to keep proper score, production control (takt) boards must also be in place and in use!

Now just because we have empowered our teams to move to, address, and resolve production flow constrains does not mean that we have abdicated our roles as managers and supervisors. Communication, instructions, training, materials, components, quality controls, production controls, disciplinary actions, production schedule adherence, on-time delivery, and more, are still our responsibilities and accountabilities as production managers and supervisors.

Empower your production associates. Empower your line teams. Allow them to support our total minute-by-minute production flow control success as we as production managers and supervisors support our production associates to move to, address, and resolve production flow constraints.

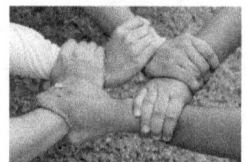

g. The Shortest Distance Between Two Points (I's, U's, L's, J's, C's, N's):

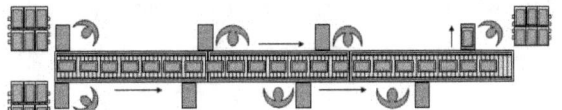

It has been said that the shortest distance between two points is a straight line . . . . and sometimes that is true. However, at other times, the shortest distance between us and effective production control and work flow management may take on a different shape! Why is that the case?

Let's consider for a moment that it is possible for a straight production line to be so long that the associate at the beginning cannot see what is happening at the end of the production process. Then, if they needed to assist in addressing and resolving a constraint, the walk times to get to and from become an inhibitor as well as a possible constraint in and of themselves.

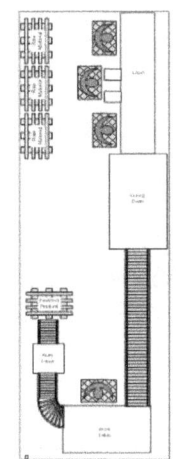

There are a number of factors to consider in total production line design structure:

1. product size, shape, and/or construction complexity,
2. required WIP levels,
3. materials queuing needs,
4. staffing level relative to scheduled output,
5. equipment types,
6. equipment availability,
7. layout / floor space availability,
8. finished product staging,
9. batch / lot QA acceptance,
10. or other factors,

that determine whether "I", "U", "T", "S", "L", "J", "C", or "N" is the appropriate line configuration structure shape.

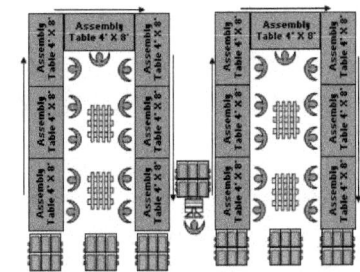

One of the key structural selection criteria must be the line-of-sight relative to the entire process in term of what the production associate can see and monitor. Next, we must determine which shape best facilitates speed and ease of move from one work station to another. Our goal is to have empowered associates freely moving to address and resolve production flow constraints on a minute-by-minute basis.

h. Continuous Improvement:

"One must be willing to accept the simple fact that we all have imperfections and we will need to work continually to become better than we were yesterday."
The Leadership Secrets of Attila the Hun

The philosophy of continuous improvement is at the very core of all total quality management, six-sigma, and/or any other sound business management philosophy. In our core values statement for management and supervision we sincerely believe and adhere to the following:

"We must experiment with new ideas. Innovation must be embraced, progressive programs developed, new methods deployed, and new services introduced. When we operate according to these principles, we will promote continued success."

We must all strive in every way to be determined to be better tomorrow than we were yesterday. Management and engineering cannot do it alone. Each and every associate within the organization must be constantly focusing upon and suggesting new and innovative ways to reduce waste, scrap, rework, error, mishap, and any other area of lost opportunity.

Management, supervision, and engineering must be open to all practical suggestions that expose waste, error, and lost opportunity and willing to pursue experimentation, testing, pilot programs, evaluations, market research, customer focus groups, and deployment of new methodologies, equipment and processes.

No matter how good we think that we might be, there will always be room for improvement. If we ever stop innovating and improving and rest on our laurels, then we are simply giving the competition an excellent opportunity to catch up!

> "Even if you are on the right track, you'll get run over if you just sit there."
>
> Will Rogers

The competitive marketplace for any product or service is a most dynamic, ever-changing, progressive environment. If you stand still long enough, the competition will eventually catch up, and might even run over you! In their book, *Re-engineering the Corporation*, Michael Hammer and James Campy well state,

> "**. . . the lowest price, the highest quality, and the best service available . . . becomes the standard for all competitors. Adequate is no longer good enough.**"

Benchmarks, standards of performance, along with customer expectations rise. The skills and capabilities of our competitors improve and advance. So what do we do? An organization must continue to advance, improve, and progressively move forward in the development of new markets, strategies, tactics, tools, and their application faster and more effectively than the competition. In his book, *The Fifth Discipline*, Peter Senge describes the "learning organization." In essence, that is an organization, or entity or business group within a larger organization that learns and deploys that learning *faster*, than its competitors. The ability to learn and make market application of that learning is in and of itself a key strategic competitive advantage. All of us within the organization must set upon a course of progressive, continuing education for ourselves and all of our associates at all critical operational levels. We must experiment with new ideas. Innovation must be embraced, new programs developed, new methods deployed, and new services introduced as the primary result of this strategic educational initiative.

Not only at an organizational level, at the individual level as well, everyone must fully embrace a continuous learning philosophy and culture. There is an old adage that the burden of responsibility for learning is not on the teacher, it is upon the student. We must all become perpetual students in regard to our specific fields of professional expertise. What characterizes a profession? Is it not that it comprises a specific and well defined set of skills and attributes that often require years of training and application to develop? Is this not often a lifelong endeavor? Also, in many instances, are not people's work lives impacted by the application of these specific skills and attributes?

The next time you board a plane consider . . . When do you suppose was the last time those professional commercial pilots engaged in a professional skills maintenance or development program? How would you feel if you knew it has been quite some years? Not too good I'll bet! How about us? How long has it been since we have addressed advancement of our management competencies? Individual's work lives and livelihoods are significantly impacted by the application of our professional leadership and managerial capabilities.

The focus of the individual leader and manager should be on the need for specific applied strategies in personal leadership attribute and managerial skill development. However, let's briefly address a key distinction between leadership and management.

We may define leadership as an identifiable set of individual attributes that through their evident demonstration and consistent application, people are *positively influenced* in a desired and appropriate direction for the common good of our customers, our organization, and individuals within it.

We may define management as skilled *guidance, direction, analysis, and control* of specific items or issues. This would encompass labor costs, products, materials, inventories, overhead, facilities, equipment, turnover, hiring, training, customer service, etc. as the focus of applied human energies.

As professional managers and leaders we must also view ourselves as an output source - the supplier or provider - of a wide range of support services to a broad range of internal and external customers. Those customers or recipients of the 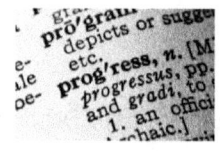 managerial and leadership services you provide range from your direct reports to the end users of the specific products and services our organization provides. Just as a skilled professional manager would well adopt a philosophy of continuous improvement regarding their own organization or respective functional area, that same individual must adopt a philosophy of continuous, ongoing improvement for themselves as a professional manager and leader. This would specifically focus upon 1) the maintenance of existing skills, 2) the development of new skills, 3) and the effective application of those skills.

To achieve your desired targets and objectives, your expertise must be effectively applied in regard to focusing and directing the effort and energy of your work force upon customer-centered as well as business plan goal attainment. If this is not done, you as the responsible manager, in all likelihood, will not succeed long-term. Just as you depend upon those professional pilots, our people depend upon *us as professionals*, for information, guidance, instruction, resources, performance feedback, trust, communication, affirmation, commendation, and much more.

As with any professional, a well-defined program of organizational and individual development and continuous improvement must be strongly and proactively pursued as markets, customer requirements, government regulations, and workplace environments change and advance. Organizational and managerial capabilities must also advance. Our leadership and managerial capabilities must keep pace. Today's skills will be obsolete tomorrow. For us collectively as an organization, as well as the individuals within it, we must totally embrace a discipline of continuous education in conjunction with market and operational deployment of that learning for us to succeed today, as well as assure our continuing success tomorrow.

Identification & Training Of Best Methods

7. Identification & Training of Best Methods:

a. Management, Supervision, and Engineering Define Methodology:

Our management, supervision, and engineering team all work to combine the requirements of the customer, the need for accuracy, the need for safety, the need for ergonomic efficiency, the requirements of OSHA, as well as the availability of equipment and facilities to produce a comprehensive methodology that will meet or exceed all of the of these combined requirements. This is accomplished in a working and collaborative operational partnership. It is not always easy!

Unfortunately, it is too often the case that the inmates are running the asylum! Singular associates are left to devise their own ways of doing things and what may be "easy" for them individually, may be making things more difficult and costly downstream. It is easy and convenient for an upstream city to dump their non-treated sewage into the river, however, what issues does that create for those other towns and other people downstream. The entire process and each operational segment within the process must be structured to facilitate to optimum efficiency for the "entire" process.

As Dr. Deming so well pointed out that total maximization of any singular process segment will result in the sub-optimization of the entire process. A balanced engineering approach must be taken in which a key focus is the total impact of each process step on the subsequent process, as well as maintaining a focus upon total process optimization. Can an associate working within the confines of their own work space and singular needs address this need for total process scope and capability? Not hardly!

That is not to say that the views, suggestions, recommendations, and participation of experienced production associates isn't needed, welcomed, appreciated, solicited, and utilized at every opportunity.
However, of primary importance is that the associates' inputs are combined within the total context of that of the entire production management, engineering, supervisory, quality assurance, and production associate group to produce a total

methodology solution that will serve the collective needs of the entire process and its resulting outputs, as well as each individual operational segment of the process.

As my Dad used to tell me,

"All of us are smarter than any of us."

By working within the structure of a collective, concerted, and focused team upon our goal of structuring a process that will yield maximum effectiveness and efficiency is a key strategy to success. Our collective intellect, creativity, experience, resourcefulness, talents, skills, and capabilities surpass genius!

b. Define Best Methods and Practices . . . Who and Where Are the Highest Levels of Total Accuracy and Productivity:

"Production is not the application of tools to material, but logic to work."
Peter Drucker

Let's first of all agree that the best is not simply the fastest! Remember the hare? He was fast, however, he lost the race. Our finish line is the end of the shift and the end of the week. Or score is the total number of first quality billable units produced at the shift's end and collectively at the week's end.

Let's also keep in mind that the most inefficient way to do anything is "over again!" The most expensive way to do anything is "on overtime." In a typical industrial environment, it generally take five times as long to do it over again, as it would have had it been done right the first time . . . yes five (5) times $$$!

While that may seem incredible at first, look at it this way. Items will need to be pulled from inventory, opened, inspected, sorted, dismantled, repaired / reworked, re-assembled, re-inspected, re-packaged, and re-inventoried. In addition, there are the additional costs of the additional packaging utilized, other additional components and/or materials consumed, and units that perhaps were damaged during the rework process and had to be scrapped $$$.

There are additional, less readily identifiable costs incurred as well. Delays and/or short-shipments creating customer dissatisfaction. The additional management time and attention required to manage the process and the documentation requirements of all the activity described in the above paragraph. Combine all this and tremendous costs have been incurred.

We must consider and focus upon the development of a balanced methodology that will yield the optimum results in efficient utilization of process labor costs and minimization of error, rework, and mishap costs. In conjunction with this focus, it must also be considered that the methodology developed must be trainable to the average / typical production associate. The ideal associate profile should not include qualifications and capabilities such as "faster than a speeding bullet, more powerful than a locomotive, and able to leap tall buildings in a single bound!" The methods that we develop must be teachable and trainable to a broad work force population which in turn 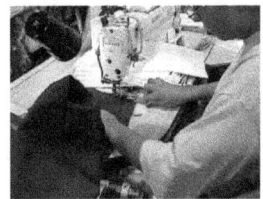 can perform the prescribed tasks with high levels of accuracy and sustainability. We must assure that by applying the methodologies that we develop and deploy that our production associates have every opportunity to succeed. When our production associated succeed, we succeed, and our customers succeed!

I summary, the "best method" first and foremost assures complete associate safety. It next provides for the optimum economic balance of accuracy, materials utilization, ergonomic efficiency, equipment performance maximization, and lastly . . . . speed!

c. Train the Best Methods and Practices . . . Mentor Training:

Let's for a moment consider that we want to learn to fly a plane. We can be an avoid student of aviation history. We can know all there is to know about aviation mechanics and electronics. We can read every book in the library on flying. However, in order to get our pilot's license, we must be thoroughly trained by a certified and qualified flight instructor.

The same is true for the production associate. You can observe, study, read, etc., however, the most applicable and effective training is provide with and through other experienced production associates. Just like we must learn flying from an experienced pilot, a production associate best learns and applies the correct operational methodology with and through another experienced production associate that has demonstrated consistency, productivity, accuracy, and reliability over some period of time, by mean of applying the correct methodologies.

Just as in sports, the best players do not necessarily make the best coaches and trainers. In the area of production associate training, the "fastest" production associates so not necessarily make the best mentor trainers. Select the best teachers / trainers from among the work force in order to best train and grow the new and expanding work force.

d. Positive Reinforcement of Progress and Achievement:

In his book, "Getting Things Done," Michael Leboeuf reviews the training process of a performing killer whale much like Shamu at Sea World. The whale at this point knows nothing about how to entertain a crowd in regard to jumping out of the water, doing some impressive acrobatics, then splashing back into the pool and drenching the first several rows with water!

The training process begins very simply with a bar lying on the bottom of the pool. Each time the killer whale swims over the bar, the trainer gives the whale a fish. The whale soon figures out that this is a good deal!

The bar is then raised a few feet above the floor of the pool. The whale again swims over the bar. Again, the trainer gives the whale a fish . . . a good deal! However, a whale swimming over a bar just above the floor of the pool doesn't do much to impress the crowd. So the bar is progressively raised, step by step, up to the top of the water. The whale now has to jump just a little to get over the bar. Again, the whale gets a fish as a reward and as the trainer and the whale grow their bond and relationship, the trainer gives the whale some stroking.

This process of progressive goal setting, positive recognition, and positive reinforcement continues unit the whale soars into the air, goes over the bar, and splashes back into the water drenching the first several rows . . . and then gives everyone a wave with his flipper!

We as humans work in much the same manner. As leaders, managers, and supervisors, we must set realistically attainable goals for our people. Then as these goals are achieved, we recognize the progress attained, positively and tangibly reward and reinforce the accomplishment, and then establish a new target. The same is true in regard to training a whale, an athlete, or a work force; set progressively attainable goals, recognize and reward the achievement of the goals, and then set new ones.

Positive Reinforcement / Celebrate Success

8. Positive Reinforcement / Celebrate Success:

a. **Effective Establishment and Communication of Appropriate Key Performance Indicators (KPI's) / Critical Success Factors & Goals:**

"The greatest thing in this world is not so much where we stand as in what direction we are going."

Oliver Wendell Holmes

There is a proverb that says, "No wind blows in favour of a ship without a destination." With their goal or destination clearly defined, yet well out of sight, the captain and crew of our ship plot a course, supply and equip the vessel, and sail out of the harbour into the open sea with their course set straight for their destination. In addition, the pilot and navigator must make periodic course adjustments and corrections as the pressures of changing winds and currents tend to force their ship off its course and away from their intended destination. The ship will require some maintenance along the way as well. Unless some unanticipated or unforeseen disaster is encountered, our ship, or for that matter almost any ship, will successfully reach its port of call, and the majority of the time, arrive on schedule.

Now, what if you took that same ship just started the engines, with no captain or crew on board, with just whatever provisions there happened to be on hand, pointed our ship in the general direction of our planned destination, and let it go? You would be doing very well if your ship even got out of the harbour. Most likely, your ship will run aground, end up on the rocks, or capsize and sink.

How are you managing your business, your career, or your profession? Have you just started your engines, pointed yourself in a general direction, and just let go and hoped for the best? Or have you set and established a specific destination, a goal or set of goals, set a defined course, and then made the necessary plans, acquired the necessary resources, and if required, developed the skills needed to reach your targeted destination on schedule.

Earl Nightingale has well-defined success as "the progressive realization of a worthy ideal." Those who are successful in life often have something in common. They have established for themselves a destination, a goal; set a course; developed a plan for their lives, in both the personal and professional arenas. Once you decide upon a profitable and worthwhile goal toward which to work, you have become a successful person. Successful individuals have a game plan for their personal and professional life.

Sadly, many people believe that they are outer-directed, that they are the victims of circumstance. We must be victors over circumstance, not the victims of it. The pressures and random occurrences of life will force you into the life and job in which you, often in frustration, may find yourself.

Therefore, you must establish realistic, measurable, and obtainable goals. If you are to become successful in whatever endeavours you wish to pursue, this is the first, and perhaps most important ingredient. You as a human are by nature goal  oriented or goal seeking, whether you realize it or not. You can either be motivated by and work toward the goals you have established for yourself, or have the goals of others imposed upon you. It has been said that those that do not have goals are destined to work for and serve those that do.

Once you have set a goal which you plan to achieve, and train your focus on that goal, then you will begin to move in the direction of that goal automatically. Earl Nightingale well said, "We are, and we become, what we think about." In addition, Dr. Dennis Waitley has similarly related, "We move in the direction of our currently dominant thoughts." Ralph Waldo Emerson similarly said, "A man is what he thinks about all day long."

Smart Goals:
The first step in the attainment of any worthwhile endeavour begins by establishing the goal. If your goals are vague, incomplete, non-specific, or unrealistic, you will not be able to properly focus upon them. You cannot effectively relate to goals such as health, wealth, happiness, or contentment.

Your goals must be "smart." Goals must be Specific, Measurable, Attainable,

Rational, and Time-framed, in order to affect you in a positive, progressive, and a motivational manner. Goals must be specific, exact, concrete, and tangible. If your goal is not something that is concrete, tangible, and measurable, then how are you going to know when you have achieved it? Our human goal-oriented system does respond to increasing your income 30%, owning a new home, running a mile in less than six minutes, obtaining a professional title, achieving a recognized level of performance attainment, or taking next year's vacation in some exotic location. These specific targets will set natural goal-seeking responses in motion.

Goals must in some manner be measurable. This could be in dollars, percentages, or improvement made verses a baseline. This measurement should be in writing also. How can you gauge your progress along the way to the achievement of your goals if they are not measurable?

Goals should be attainable in that they are out of your grasp but not beyond your reach. An unrealistic or otherwise unattainable goal often serves as a de-motivator and can be a source of frustration.

Goals must be rational in that they serve a constructive and meaningful purpose in relation to you, your people, the organization, your customers, and the community. Why achieve a goal if it does not serve the common good?

Goals must be time-framed in that there is a realistic and identified target date for the attainment of the goal. This greatly contributes to establishing appropriate priorities.

Now some people may say that they don't want making a lot of money as their goal, but a person that would say that would probably lie about other things too. You, in some instances, may use money in relation to a goal, but this is done simply as a means of measurement in regard to that goal's attainment. Since you move in the direction of our currently dominant thoughts and thereby become what you think about most of the time, then no wonder so many individuals fail to live up to their full potential.

As you become what you think about, if you have no goals, if you have not set a direction, then the result will be frustration, fear, anxiety, worry, and failure. If you focus on nothing, you become nothing. If your personal and professional goals are just "tension-relieving" instead of "goal-achieving," then you will accomplish little or nothing at all.

No one wants to be a failure. No one wants to be mediocre. No one wants a life filled with worry, fear, anxiety, and frustration. No one I know routinely gets up out of bed in the morning and loudly proclaims, "I'm going to be a failure today!" You avoid these things by setting for yourself and others clear, precise, profitable goals. Whether you lead a successful life or a failed one, it takes just about the same amount of energy and effort either way. The person who succeeds is the one who is working toward a worthy ideal, a goal. As you work toward the attainment, the fulfillment of your goals, then such things as anxiety, worry, doubt, and fear will tend to have less of an effect upon you.

Your goals must also be compatible with each other, working in concert with, and not against, each other. Your goals must also be in full and complete harmony with all natural laws, all physical laws and all moral laws. Remember, you are what you think about, so in order to control your personal and professional life, then you must control the focus of your mental and physical energy.

You should also realize that many of your limitations are self-imposed. You have many opportunities before you if you will set goals for yourself, keep them constantly in front of you, and concentrate upon them every day. Stop thinking about your fears, your anxieties, and your worries. Instead, replace these negative mental images by focusing upon a clear mental picture of the goals that you are working to achieve.

Now don't immediately begin to overly concern yourself with just exactly how you are going to go about achieving your goals. The first and most important thing that must be determined is *where* you are going. As you concentrate and focus on your goals, action plans to support the attainment of those goals will begin to take shape in time.

Money as a Goal:
If you set for yourself a goal of increasing your income, know that the only

people who make money, are those who work in a mint. You, like the rest of us must earn money. You have to work for it. You must make a meaningful and valued contribution to humanity in some form or fashion. If you want to increase our income, then you must increase your contribution in relation to the products and services you provide.

You exchange your time, your mental and physical energy, your product, or your services, for the other person's money. Your financial reward will be in

direct proportion to the service you render. Success is not making money. Making money is the result of success. Your success will be in direct proportion to our contribution in terms of the quality and quantity of the products or services you provide through the application of your mental and physical energy. If you want to earn more, contribute more.

As you stand in front of the stove of life, you must first put the wood in, before you can get any heat out. You must provide a product or service of value first, then financial rewards will come to you. Therefore, you must set your goals accordingly, in harmony with the law of mutual exchange.

Setting Goals:
A goal is just a wish, a dream, a fantasy, until you *put them in writing*! Establish clear, measurable goals, and then commit them to hard copy. List the rewards and benefits that will result from the achievement of your goals. Establish long-range, five years or longer goals, intermediate one-year goals, and short-range monthly goals. Set a definite time frame in which you will attain your goals. Recognize and list the obstacles and challenges that must be overcome before attaining your goals. Identify the people who can aid and assist you to meet the challenges faced as you progressively work to reach our goals. List the skills and abilities that you have as well as those you will need to develop or acquire, in order to realize your goals. Develop daily objectives, a daily "to-do" list. In the manner you will develop the detailed step-by-step plan that must be executed; the course to be followed, progressively and systematically, that will ultimately lead to the attainment of your goals.

Goals & Stress:

Market changes, sickness, family problems, accidents, government regulation, these things do occur. By focusing on your goals, the enthusiasm of accomplishment, of achievement, of attaining that goal, this will enable you to determinedly persist through any difficult or trying period. As you remain calm, cheerful, and positive, focusing on your goals, the petty trials and annoyances of life won't get you off course.

You can act promptly and decisively when your plan, your course, is defined and clear. When negative fearful thoughts begin to trigger your stress response, stop them by focusing instead upon the achievement, the realization of your goals. As you keep your goals clearly in view, then you will be better able to make whatever adjustments are necessary, more effectively deal with pressures and difficulties as they arise, as you remain focused upon your objectives. You will continue to move progressively toward their accomplishment.

Goals have also been compared to the rudder of a ship. Are you and your organization a ship without a rudder? Are you being steered by the random winds and currents of life? Are you hoping that random chance will bring you to your desired destination? The overwhelming probability is that this will not happen. You must decide for yourself where it is you are going. Then you must set the goals, develop the necessary plans, and set the specific course you are to follow, and make whatever course adjustments are necessary along the way.

Your goals give you purpose, focus, and direction. Decide what it is that you want to accomplish with your time, mental and physical energy, your talents and assets, rather than waiting for things to *take* your time, energy, and assets. Secure your advantage, effectively direct your energies, assure your success, and establish goals.

Goals & Peak Performance:

A common malady is that sometimes you forget what it is that you have set out to do. You need written, well-defined goals. You are surrounded by pressures, distractions, and stressors that get you off course. The best defences you have are written goals and objectives that serve to keep you focused and on course. The main purpose for setting goals is to give you control over your lives and your work.

"The best way to predict the future is to create it."

Peter Drucker

The best way to predict the future is to create it by means of progressive goal setting. Brian Tracy states, "The day you begin working from clear written goals, organized by priority, is the day you begin moving toward peak performance in your career." With the ever-accelerating rate of change that you must face in the work place today, you may feel a loss of control, and in turn, this increases the stress level you experience. You may feel as if you are being manipulated by external forces that you cannot influence and therefore you cannot determine your future. However, as you establish goals, objectives, and action plans, and then write them down, you regain a measure of control and authority over your own destiny.

All high achieving men and women are goal oriented. They have committed their goals to paper and have developed detailed plans to achieve these goals. After decades of studying and speaking on success, Brian Tracy has concluded that . . .

"Goal setting is the master skill of success. It is more important to become a skilled goal-setter than it is to develop any other ability."

The more precise and specific your goals can be, the greater the probability of their achievement. However, if your goals are vague or ill defined, then your results will likewise be unclear or blurry. Be clear about exactly what it is that you want to accomplish. The critical factor is that you now feel more in control of your own destiny.

You must also be willing to discipline yourself to put forth the effort required to work progressively and persistently toward the attainment of your goals. You must be willing to discipline yourself to put forth the sustained effort required to achieve success.

The first question you need to ask yourself is, "How can I increase my personal productivity, my individual contribution?" You should ask yourself these questions. "Why am I on the payroll? What results have I been hired to achieve? (Focus on **results**, not activities.) Why is my department on the customer's payroll? What results are we hired to achieve for our customers?"

An important point to keep in mind is that your customer is the person or persons whose level of satisfaction directly determines your level of success. Who is that? Who is the consumer of your product or service? Your co-workers? Your staff? The answer is, your immediate superior! He or she is your most important customer in that your rate of success or failure is in extremely large part determined by their level of satisfaction in relation to the results that you achieve.

So, sit down and make a list of everything you feel that you have been hired to accomplish. Ask your superior to help you put everything in appropriate priority order. For you to maximize your opportunity for success in your job, you must fully comprehend the goals and objectives of your superior and then incorporate their goals into your own goals.

In order to afford them the optimum opportunity for accomplishment, your staff likewise needs to have their accountabilities, objectives, and goals clearly defined for them as well. As their supervisor, your staff deserves to know exactly what results they have been hired to achieve, to what levels of quality, and in what time frames.

Unless your people are successful, as their supervisor or manager, you cannot be successful unless they are. The first and most important element involved in their success is to provide them with clear, precise, measurable goals. As you do so, their opportunity, and yours, to achieve, excel, and succeed, will be greatly enhanced.

Business Goal Setting:

Following are the key result areas that are crucial for business success. Whether you are an employee, a manager, or the owner of a business, the following key business performance areas significantly relate to total business success and therefore should well be considered in your goal setting exercise. These goals must be clearly defined, well communicated, and understood by all in the organization to whom they apply. Goals established in these areas must also be specific, measurable, attainable, rational, and time-framed. You must be clear about what needs to be accomplished. Then concentrate and focus energies and assets upon the areas that will yield the maximum results. This is no more important in any other instance than these few key result areas.

Productivity:

Think of yourself as a factory with inputs of labor, raw materials, and energy, and outputs or results. You must constantly be striving to increase your output, the results you achieve, what you accomplish, in relation to your inputs, the inputs of your mental and physical energy. Strive continually to increase your personal productivity.

Customer Satisfaction:

"If we don't take care of the customer, somebody else will."

Anonymous

We have reviewed the importance of recognizing your superior as your most important customer. Next comes your staff, the individuals whose activities you direct and influence. In order for them to produce at their peak levels, then you as their manager must work to create an environment in which your staff can feel comfortable and thereby productive.

Your next most important customer is the person or persons that are the immediate users of what you produce and/or the services that you provide. This may be the external customer, the final consumer. You must admit that none of us would likely be employed if it were not for the final consumer.

Our customer could also be an internal customer. These are the people that must use information, a part or component, anything that you and your functional area have produced. They add to, continue, or further advance the product or process that you have begun. Within your organization, anyone that uses your output in the performance of his or her respective job duties is your internal customer.

All targets and goals must be in total alignment with those of our client company and/or the products purchaser / end-users. Our Key Performance Indicators (KPI's) must also be their Key Performance Indicators (KPI's).

We need to concern ourselves with how we can continually improve. Ask your internal and external customers what they need to be fully satisfied with what you accomplish and how you can do more for them.

Profitability:

In order to continue to thrive, grow, innovate, expand in its market, and provide for the continued security of its employees, a business must be profitable. How can you make increased company profitability a meaningful goal? It is helpful to understand the relationship between costs, sales dollars, and profits. For example, in the typical sales dollar there may be 10 cents or so of actual profit. Therefore, an increase in sales of $10 dollars will yield a $1 dollar of increased bottom-line profit. However, if you reduce operating or production costs by $1 dollar, then that will in turn add a $1 full dollar of profit to the bottom line, with no increase in sales revenue.

So ask yourself, "What can I do to control or reduce costs? How can I make a contribution to improved company profitability by reducing operating expenses?" As company profitability is improved, this in turn can well contribute to improved job security as well as enhanced pay and benefits.

Quality:

The marketplace today is demanding quality in virtually every area in regard to products and services. Only the quality leaders will survive. Your concern must be the quality of your product or service, the quality of the output of your functional area, and the quality of your personal work. You should strive to establish "smart" goals in these areas to the extent practical. To maximize your opportunities for continued success, you should adopt the philosophy of "zero defects." That doesn't mean that you should expect that you will never make a defect, error, or mistake. It means that you should set for yourself, and those you influence, a goal of **continuous improvement**, always pursuing avenues, setting goals for improvement in your product, service, or personal work.

Human Development:
People produce their best results when they feel good about themselves and those with whom they work. You can positively influence those who work either with you or for you by giving them praise, encouragement, and positive support. Treat your fellow workers with dignity, respect, courtesy, honesty, empathy, and understanding. Establish goals in regard to helping and supporting the people you work with, to build their morale, and achieve their best. Consider goals such as completion of specific development or training courses, attainment of advancement opportunities, as well as absenteeism and turnover. People accomplish worthwhile results when they feel good about themselves, their company, and the other people with whom they work.

Organizational Development:
This key result area consists of planning, organizing, training, developing, delegating, measuring, and reporting. Your organization, as it moves forward under today's market and financial conditions, will require monitoring and controlling. In addition, when required, the organization will need modification, development, and innovative approaches as it responds to the ever-changing environments in which business is conducted. In order to insure the best possible opportunities for success, goals must be set that relate to the establishment and maintenance of an internal organizational structure that will appropriately respond to external market and financial forces.

Innovation:
The vital need to progress, to enhance the results you achieve, and to better satisfy your internal and external customers is constantly ongoing. Many companies today have instituted such programs as "Total Employee Involvement," "Opportunities for Improvement," "Corrective Action Teams," and "Continuous Process Improvement, "Lean Manufacturing, ""Six Sigma."

All these, as well as other similar programs, recognize the importance of the full participation of all the employees in the organization, and at all levels, in the efforts required to achieve the necessary goals of progressive improvement, positive change, and advancing innovation. Your goal should be to contribute your thoughts, ideas, suggestions, and other constructive inputs, as well as encourage those within your area of responsibility to contribute their thoughts, ideas, suggestions, and other constructive inputs into the efforts focused upon increased cost effectiveness, quality improvement, and enhanced customer satisfaction.

Conclusion:
Goals are the key ingredients to a productive, rewarding, and successful life, career, and business. Assure yourself and your organization an advantage as

you pursue prosperity and accomplishment. Establish your destination; establish your direction; move continuously, progressively, and straightforward toward the achievement of your goals. What are the most vital goals for you? You must develop them for yourself, your functional area, or your company.

Unleash the power for achievement as you focus human efforts and energies upon the goals you wish to attain for the benefit of our customers, the organization, your people, and you.

b. **Establish Cognitive Dissonance . . . Track and Communicate Actual Performance Verses Goal:**

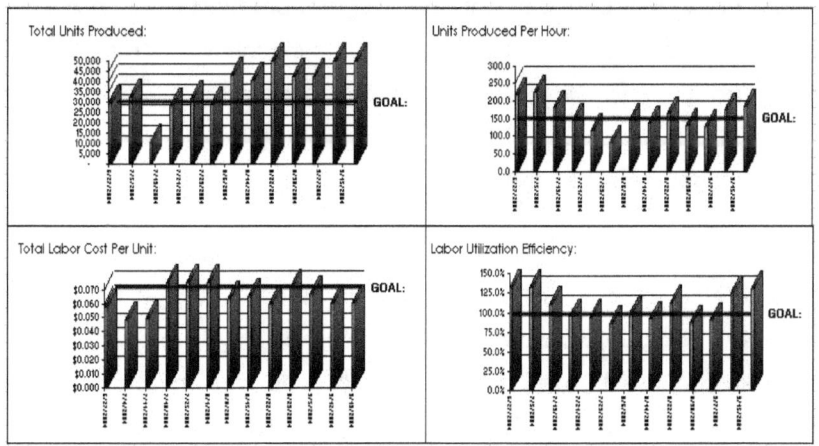

I will always remember my first visit to one of the world's preeminent performance textile manufacturers, Milliken. In each and every production area, the critical production success factors / key performance indicators were highly visible as they were displayed upon very large graph boards. These display board could be clearly seen and read from virtually every part of the production area. The specific performance goal was clearly indicated as well as progress toward or away from the targeted goal was clearly tracked for all to see. An additional thing that I also noticed was that the overwhelming majority of the CSF / KPI measurements were all moving in a positive direction.

Everyone naturally desires to be a winner. To achieve and succeed in the areas that promote the success of the team, the organization, the customer, and themselves. No one wants to be a failure!

There is a physiological principle that we can put into play and that is cognitive dissonance. We do not like to hear or see audibly nor visibly sour notes. As humans, we feel good as we have confirmation that we are moving in a positive and beneficial direction. We do not like it when it is likewise confirmed to us that we are moving in a negative and potentially harmful direction. If at all possible, we are going to do something about it!

This principle may be applied in the areas of production out volume, executional accuracy, defect percentages, materials utilization, on-time delivery, efficiency, spending control, virtually any production performance area that can be measured, tracked, and wherein the work force have a direct impact upon the levels of performance attained.

"Things that get measured, get done."

Peter Drucker

The targeted goal is the result that we must achieve to assure our collective success. The graph indicated movement either toward or away from critical, key results. It have been said that, "Feedback is the breakfast of champions." It is vital that we as managers and supervisors provide accurate and timely production performance feedback in clear, concise, and easily interpreted structures. In that way, our production associates can and will become production performance champions!

c. Set Up the Win . . . Celebrate Success!

Once we have these accurate and timely performance feedback structures in place, (highly visible KPI targets, graphs, and charts) we have also established a vehicle that allows us as managers and supervisors to provide positive reinforcement in regard to key results attainment.

As Dr. Ken Blanchard so well states in his classic book, "The One-Minute Manager,"

"Catch people doing things right!"

Recognize meaningful achievement in relation to KPI target attainment or significant progress, then offer sincere praise. This can be in the form of a sincere thanks for a job well done. It can be a job related gift, award, certificate, dinner or other type of recognition. The key element is to bring into the working environment the feeling of satisfaction that comes from a job well done and that well done job is recognized and rewarded by management and supervision. The response of the work force will be to continue to achieve and to move toward even greater levels of success. All we in management and supervision need to do is catch our people doing the right things right, and then recognizing and rewarding them for it.

d. Raise the Bar:

One must be willing to accept the simple fact that we all have imperfections and we will need to work continually to become better than we were yesterday.

> Taken from "The Leadership Secrets of Attila the Hun"

Our first goal was to ride our bike with the training wheels on. The next goal was to remove those training wheels as soon as possible. Our next goal was to see just how fast and/or how far we could go!

We should view our production performance in much the same way. We may need to start with the training wheels on, however, we want to get them off as soon as possible and then start working to see how fast and how far we can go.

Once a specified level of production performance has been achieved and maintained for a reasonable period, now let's see if we can go a little farther and/or a little faster. Raise the performance bar just a little. Progressive goal setting must be incremental. If we push too far or too fast we might fall with resulting injury to ourselves or others. As with setting SMART goals remember that the "A" is "attainable." Raise goals in an incrementally and be certain to avoid a targeted goal being a source of frustration.

This progressive, incremental of raising our production performance targets provides the foundation for the continuous improvement process. If we never pushed progressively forward, how would we ever get better? We also must always remember that the competition is always hard at work. We must continuously improve or the competition will eventually catch up and pass us!

Raise the bar, establish progressive performance targets, and continuously improve!

e. Do It All Over Again!

"The beacons of productivity and innovation must be our guideposts. If we _continue to improve productivity_ of all key resources and our innovative standing, we are going to be profitable."

Peter Drucker

The competition never sleeps. Markets are ever changing. Customer requirements and needs are constantly increasing. We must learn progress, develop, and grow faster than the competition.

Now that we have it all complete, in place, and well-functioning, we must ask and explore . . . how can we do better, advance, and improve. We must raise the bar for ourselves and move to ever improving levels  of delivery, quality, and cost performance and maintain our competitive position and continue to win!

All information contained in this publication is the exclusive and proprietary property of William. R. Puckett. Any duplication or reproduction in any manner whatsoever, without expressed written consent is strictly prohibited.

Copyright Application 1-TNS4ZV – October 2nd, 2014

www.ingramcontent.com/pod-product-compliance
Lightning Source LLC
Chambersburg PA
CBHW051718170526
45167CB00002B/708